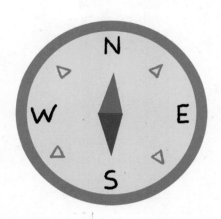

No More Random Acts of Literacy Coaching

Dear Readers,

Much like the diet phenomenon Eat This, Not That, this series aims to replace some existing practices with approaches that are more effective—healthier, if you will—for our students. We hope to draw attention to practices that have little support in research or professional wisdom and offer alternatives that have greater support. Each text is collaboratively written by authors representing research and practice. Section 1 offers practitioner perspective(s) on a practice in need of replacing and helps us understand the challenges, temptations, and misunderstandings that have led us to this ineffective approach. Section 2 provides researcher perspective(s) on the lack of research to support the ineffective practice(s), and reviews research supporting better approaches. In Section 3, the author(s) representing practitioner perspective(s) give detailed descriptions of how to implement these better practices. By the end of each book, you will understand both what not to do, and what to do, to improve student learning.

It takes courage to question one's own practice—to shift away from what you may have seen throughout your years in education and toward something new that you may have seen few, if any, colleagues use. We applaud you for demonstrating that courage and wish you the very best in your journey from this to that.

Best wishes,
— *M. Colleen Cruz* and *Nell K. Duke, Series Editors*

NOT THIS BUT THAT

No More
Random Acts of
Literacy Coaching

ERIN BROWN AND SUSAN K. L'ALLIER

HEINEMANN
PORTSMOUTH, NH

Heinemann

361 Hanover Street

Portsmouth, NH 03801–3912

www.heinemann.com

Offices and agents throughout the world

The authors and publisher wish to thank those who have generously given permission to reprint borrowed material:

Figure 2–1: Adapted from "Standards 2017 Overarching Standards" from the International Literacy Association's website: https://literacyworldwide.org/get-resources/standards/standards-2017, accessed July 10, 2020. Copyright © 2017 by the International Literacy Association. Reprinted by permission of the International Literacy Association.

Credit lines continue on page x.

Library of Congress Cataloging-in-Publication Data

Names: Brown, Erin, author. | L'Allier, Susan K., author.

Title: No more random acts of literacy coaching / Erin Brown and Susan K. L'Allier.

Description: Portsmouth, NH : Heinemann Publishing, [2020] | Includes bibliographical references.

Identifiers: LCCN 2020015132 | ISBN 9780325120089 (paperback)

Subjects: LCSH: Language arts teachers—In-service training—United States | Content area reading—United States. | Mentoring in education—United States. | Literacy—Study and teaching—United States.

Classification: LCC LB2844.1.R4 B76 2020 | DDC 418.0071—dc23

LC record available at https://lccn.loc.gov/2020015132

Series Editors: M. Colleen Cruz and Nell K. Duke

Acquisitions Editor: Margaret LaRaia

Production Editor: Sean Moreau

Cover Illustrator: James Yang

Cover and Interior Designer: Monica Ann Crigler

Typesetter: Valerie Levy, Drawing Board Studios

Manufacturing: Val Cooper

Printed in the United States of America on acid-free paper

1 2 3 4 5 6 7 8 9 10 CGB 25 24 23 22 21 20

August 2020 Printing

CONTENTS

INTRODUCTION

M. Colleen Cruz

*T*ake a few seconds to think of a great coach. This could be a famous athletic coach or one you had while playing sports growing up. If you, like me, are not really involved in traditional athletics, you might choose a coach from the field of dance, speech, or chess. What were these coaches' characteristics? How did they manage to be so successful at what they did?

Literacy coaches are often pulled in many directions, and there may be few opportunities to hone their craft. It is understandable that the work can feel random. But the best coaches think on both the macro and micro level. When I think of famously great coaches from fields other than education, I think of the meticulous, strategic planning that no doubt goes into their decisions. These coaches spend hours watching and studying videos and live practices of plays, speeches, and pirouettes. They then take those observations and produce pages upon pages of notes, diagrams, and lists to help create a cohesive plan. Everything from the warm-ups to the drills to the locker room pep talk is planned in a big picture, long-term way. Everything is planned out, from sequence of strategies and knowledge introduced to the best ways to share these ideas. Yes, of course, there is room for coaches to respond to the needs of those they are coaching and the unexpected moments that come up in the game, debate, or performance. However, there is still very much a long-term view to things so that even those seemingly spontaneous acts of coaching fall into line and are part of a larger vision.

Coaching, whether it involves basketball or literacy, can feel and look at times like it is 100 percent responsive and in the moment. Erin Brown and Susan K. L'Allier help us understand that the best coaching is not just random good luck, but rather the product of careful and expert planning and preparation. In many schools, there is a feeling that coaching is something that can be employed as a stopgap measure when and if you need it. If a teacher is new or encountering a difficult patch, we hope we can just fly a literacy coach in from the wings to save the day. This ambulance model of coaching rarely, if ever, leads to the legacy-style growth and excellence we see in longtime championship sports teams, let alone in schools.

This book challenges the notion that great coaching can't be taught. Erin and Susan don't pull any punches. They walk us through the real-world challenges and sometimes poor choices that schools can make when it comes to literacy coaching. Then they show us what studies can teach us about successful school-level literacy coaching, and then they go on to break it down into concrete, accessible steps. After spending time with hundreds of coaches in countless classrooms, I can say with confidence that the work suggested by Erin and Susan can, and does, make an impactful difference, both in literacy instructional practices and the literacy growth of students.

SECTION **1**

NOT ● THIS

In-the-Moment, For-the-Moment Coaching

SUSAN K. L'ALLIER

The role of a coach is to support teachers in meeting the needs of students. Eager to provide that support, coaches often find themselves reacting to teacher requests, such as:

"What lesson will help me teach this specific skill?"

"Can you share a good resource for phonemic awareness instruction?"

"I am supposed to give this assessment to my students this week. Can you go over the administration procedures with me?"

"Can you help me find some books that my below-grade-level readers would like?"

These random acts of support may result in one-time successes; however, they rarely have an impact on long-term student growth. We sometimes forget the research-established fact that when teachers, principals, and coaches work together to create a climate of intentional, ongoing professional learning, the likelihood of student literacy growth increases! Let's look at some of the common obstacles that can inhibit this collaborative climate.

When teachers, principals, and coaches work together to create a climate of intentional, ongoing professional learning, the likelihood of student literacy growth increases!

Teachers: "We don't need help; our students need help!"

The Obstacle: Teachers don't see coaching as a way to support student learning.

Carlotta and Elissa, two third-grade teachers, have just heard that the principal has hired a literacy coach whose main focus will be working with teachers. Carlotta and Elissa would have preferred that another reading specialist be hired to assist Paula, their current reading specialist, in providing interventions to more of their struggling readers. In sharing her thoughts with Elissa, Carlotta says, "We have so many students who need help." Carlotta agrees and adds, "I wish the principal had asked us what was needed instead of just hiring a literacy coach."

What if teachers understood how the change will support their students?

Coaching will improve core literacy instruction.

Literacy coaching is job-embedded professional development with the goal of improving core literacy instruction and student learning. When fewer than 80 percent of the students in a school are meeting or exceeding proficiency on critical literacy assessments (as is the case in Carlotta and Elissa's school), simply adding intervention time is not the answer. Core literacy instruction needs attention and support. Teaching practices and/or curricular materials used for core instruction may not be aligned to one or more of the following:

For different coaching strategies to achieve different goals, see Section 3, pages 69–73.

- learning standards,
- research-supported instructional practices,
- findings from literacy assessments, and
- areas of urgent student need.

Even when there are sufficient personnel to provide interventions, students who receive their prescribed minutes of intervention per day and then return to classrooms with misaligned core literacy instruction are unlikely to become proficient readers and writers. It will help teachers like Carlotta and Elissa to realize that when coaches, teachers, and principals work together to strengthen and differentiate core literacy instruction, the result will be improved student learning—increasing the percentage of proficient readers and reducing the number of students needing intervention.

Students who receive their prescribed minutes of intervention per day and then return to classrooms with misaligned core literacy instruction are unlikely to become proficient readers and writers.

Clear communication creates teacher buy-in for coaching.

The problem in this case isn't just with Carlotta and Elissa's perceptions, but in a lack of communication between administration and teachers. When leaders put plans in place without making their intentions clear and without inviting teachers into the thinking behind such plans, resentment and resistance are common obstacles to the necessary work of improving instruction. In their communications, administrators need to acknowledge that improving core instruction is not easy; however, achieving that goal will be possible if everyone works together to delineate the issues and develop an intentional plan to address those issues.

For strategies to increase collaboration between principals and coaches, see Section 3, pages 80–85.

Teachers: "Coaching is just one more thing to put on our plates."

The Obstacle: Teachers view coaching as yet another initiative.

Second-grade teachers Malcolm and Deidre are discussing their principal's expectations for the upcoming year: "OK, first we have our school improvement plan that has a focus on conferring with students about their progress in reading, writing, and math. Then, we are just in the second year of using a new word study program and still have a lot of learning to do about what works best for our students. And we can't forget the new social and emotional learning curriculum; we'll be attending workshops about it and then we'll need to start implementing it. Now, our principal is encouraging us to participate in the coaching program that's starting this year. There's no way we can do that, too!"

What if teachers knew that coaching would help them meet existing expectations?

A coach is someone with whom to think and problem-solve.

Coaching is not an initiative or a new program. It is a method of providing ongoing support to teachers as they navigate the daily challenges of their work. Coaches help teachers think through solutions to problems that are inhibiting student success. These problems are often associated with school-wide areas of student need and with new curricular initiatives but can also be unique to a specific teacher. When coaches think and problem-solve with a grade-level team or individual teacher, they help teachers deal with some of the numerous tasks on their instructional plates.

Coaches can support teachers in many ways.

Coaches know that adults learn best when they are involved in the planning and implementation of their learning experiences. Thus, teachers must be codesigners of the work they do with coaches. Their work together is intentional, which includes setting a goal for their collaboration and selecting the most appropriate ways to achieve that goal. For example, coaches often provide resources, co-plan and co-teach lessons, and observe specific student behaviors during lessons taught by the teacher. Coaches are sincere when they ask, "How can I best support you?" Teachers who carefully consider their responses to this question feel in control of their work with coaches—work that often helps them tackle those school-wide objectives and new initiatives.

Teacher: "I have to be careful and perform for my coach."

The Obstacle: Teachers view coaches as evaluators.

Emilio and Jasmine are walking past the office and see the coach and the principal having a meeting. Emilio says, "You know, Lavinia, our coach, was just in my room this morning and now she's meeting with the principal. I wonder if she's sharing what she saw with Mr. DeMars." Jasmine nods and adds, "Hmm, just last week, Mr. DeMars said that I might want to work with Lavinia about my shared reading lessons. I wonder if he's talking to Lavinia about my teaching."

What if teachers knew what the coach and principal talked about?

Create a shared understanding about evaluation and coaching.

Teachers are more comfortable working with coaches when principals clearly and frequently communicate that:

- the principal is the evaluator and
- the coach is the teacher's partner in planning and implementing effective teaching and learning practices.

Principals and coaches know that discussing individual teachers' needs and progress undermines teachers' trust in the confidentiality of their work with the coach. Some might think it's okay if principals and coaches discuss the successes of individual teachers. However, teachers who find out that their principal and coach are discussing teachers' successes also assume that they are discussing individual teacher needs. So, this policy of not discussing individual teachers is a critical ground rule for principals and coaches.

Coaches and principals do discuss school-wide topics.

Teachers like Emilio and Jasmine may ask, "Well, if principals and coaches do not discuss individual teachers, what do they discuss?" Coaches and principals need to carefully delineate the scope of their work, which generally focuses on school-wide topics. They often discuss school-wide data and how those results offer insights about future professional learning offerings. In addition, as coaches spend time with teachers implementing and reflecting on aspects of the literacy curriculum, it is common for coaches and principals to discuss what supports (e.g., resources, personnel, common planning time) might be needed to solve some of the school-wide curricular issues. Principals who publicly share the topics of their coach-principal meetings build teachers' confidence that the focus of those meetings is *not* the instructional practice of individual teachers.

Coach: "I feel overwhelmed and distracted by competing demands."

The Obstacle: Every coaching activity is given equal importance.

When Erin begins to mentor a group of school-based coaches, she asks them to share their schedules for the past three weeks. She frequently notes that, across the three-week period, each coach has engaged in at least twenty different coaching activities. She often sees that coaches are spending a majority of their time attending a variety of school- and district-wide meetings, planning and implementing family literacy nights, inputting assessment data, organizing book rooms, and ordering curricular materials. When these activities take over a coach's schedule, work with teachers may be limited to random, one-time interactions such as modeling a specific lesson or conferencing about a particular student. Erin notes that few coaches report involvement in ongoing coaching cycles focused on teacher practice and student learning. Many coaches share that there is just not enough time to engage in deep collaboration with each teacher and do everything else that is expected of them!

What if coaches were able to prioritize their work with teachers?

Clear, research-supported job descriptions are critical.

If you examine the job descriptions of many coaches, you will see that each includes a list of more than twenty responsibilities, many of which do not involve working directly with teachers. Coaches feel overwhelmed when they attempt to complete this long list of responsibilities, realizing that they cannot put their best effort into each task. They often report that they feel they are engaged in "random acts of coaching." Coaches can begin to alleviate this stress by working with their principals to revise their job descriptions to more closely align with the coaching activities that have been found to result in student literacy growth. This realignment will definitely increase the focus on their collaborative work with teachers. A clear, research-supported job description that is put into practice is a great first step to intentional coaching!

Coaches must make thoughtful selection of the teachers with whom they work.

It is not unusual for principals to want all teachers to receive coaching support. However, principals and coaches need to consider options for the delivery of this support. In one possible option, the coach would begin by giving one or two presentations around a specific instructional practice to all teachers, followed by grade-level and individual coaching where needed. In another possible option, the coach would work with teachers at one or two grade levels for a six-week period and then move on to other grade levels for the next six weeks and so on. Examining possible coaching approaches assumes intentional planning of the participants and the content of the coaching.

A cautionary tale: Some principals and coaches decide that the coach should work with only first- and second-year teachers or teachers who may be perceived as weaker teachers. We would caution against this as it sends the message that only certain groups of teachers would benefit from coaching. In reality, any teacher whose students are struggling with an aspect of literacy development can benefit from having someone with whom to think and problem-solve. Even very skilled teachers whose students are performing well can be involved with the coach—and are often the first people to volunteer for coaching. These teachers can frequently articulate their own professional learning goals but often want a partner to join them in planning and launching their learning adventures.

As emphasized earlier, clear communication about the specifics of the coaching program will help teachers and coaches form the partnerships needed to engage in ongoing, intentional work to increase student learning.

Principal: "After a year, the coaching program hasn't increased student achievement."

The Obstacle: Sometimes, leaders don't realize that improvement in student learning takes time.

Mrs. Gregonis, the principal of Lincoln Elementary School, has been an enthusiastic supporter of the coaching program at her school. She and her coach, Amy, carefully introduced the program to the staff; she attended almost all of Amy's professional learning sessions; and she has worked with Amy to be sure that Amy is spending most of her time working directly with teachers. However, when she looks at the end-of-the-year standardized assessments, she is seeing little change from the previous year. She thought that, after a whole year of coaching, the scores would be better. Is coaching not having an impact? Should she consider other options for professional learning next year?

What if administrators knew a little more about the change process?

Like Mrs. Gregonis, most of us want to see quick positive outcomes from our efforts. However, change does not generally happen quickly. The theory of action surrounding professional development suggests that changes in teacher knowledge and skills precede changes in student achievement. This means that during the first year of coaching, when coach-teacher relationships are just beginning to develop and intentional coaching is being put in place, it is likely that principals could see changes in teachers' instructional practices, but not changes in student achievement on standardized tests. Many of the school reform efforts that included a coaching component showed an increase in student growth over time. So, as schools embark on a second or third year of coaching, we would encourage principals to work with their coaches and teachers to expand the use of intentional coaching and to consider multiple ways to assess the impact of coaching on teacher practice and student literacy growth.

During the first year of coaching, when coach-teacher relationships are just beginning to develop and intentional coaching is being put in place, it is likely that principals could see changes in teachers' instructional practices, but not changes in student achievement on standardized tests.

In this section, we have shared some of the common obstacles that prevent teachers and coaches from engaging in intentional work around teacher and student needs. In Section 2, Susan discusses the research about effective literacy coaching. Then, in Section 3, Erin shares many examples of how teachers, coaches, and principals can collaborate to increase the use of research-supported instructional practices to improve student literacy learning. We encourage you to use the research and examples to design an intentional coaching plan that will work for your school!

SECTION **2**

WHY ● NOT?

Research Shows the Way to Intentional Coaching

SUSAN K. L'ALLIER

Not so many years ago, teachers saw their classrooms as their private domains—places where they made most of the decisions about what to teach and how to teach it. They often appeared confident that their university experiences and continuing professional learning equipped them to make decisions that would move their students forward. However, new understandings and changed expectations mean that teachers require knowledge in assessment-driven instruction, standards-based curriculum, research-supported practices, and differentiated instruction, leaving many teachers less confident about their ability to meet the needs of all their students. They may feel inundated with instructional directives and are looking for support to implement them.

Literacy coaches have the potential to provide teachers with that support. Coaches should have positive assumptions about teachers: teachers are doing their best and want to learn more about effective instructional strategies. Coaches should be non-judgmental; they see themselves as thinking partners, helping teachers address questions such as "When I think about the reading and writing I want my students to do, what gets in the way?" (Toll 2006, 36) or "When I think about all of the resources I have to teach this strategy, how do I decide which ones to use?" In this section, we examine the research that can help turn that coaching potential into reality.

As you read about the research, you will notice that coaching is often one component of a larger professional learning initiative aimed at improving student literacy achievement (e.g., Reading First [Bean et al. 2008], the Literacy Collaborative [Biancarosa, Bryk, and Dexter 2010], and Content-Focused Coaching [Matsumura et al. 2010]). Because these initiatives focus on the learning, implementation, and assessment of specific literacy instructional practices, participating coaches are likely to engage in intentional coaching around those practices—thus avoiding the random acts of coaching discussed in Section 1.

Who Is a Literacy Coach? Qualifications, Roles, and Responsibilities

If you are a literacy coach reflecting on your position, a principal preparing to hire a literacy coach, a teacher starting to work with a literacy coach, or a teacher who wants to become a literacy coach, you may be asking the following questions:

- What knowledge and skills should a literacy coach possess?
- What roles should the literacy coach play in a school?
- What are the specific responsibilities of a literacy coach?

We can turn to research and the *Standards for the Preparation of Literacy Professionals 2017* (International Literacy Association 2018) to answer these questions. Over the past sixty years, the International Literacy Association has published standards that specify the knowledge, skills, and dispositions expected of literacy professionals, including reading/literacy specialists and literacy coaches. These standards, periodically revised by literacy experts to incorporate the most recent research and address current issues and needs, serve as a guide and evaluation tool to programs that prepare literacy professionals.

What knowledge and skills should a literacy coach possess?

According to the *Standards for the Preparation of Literacy Professionals 2017* (International Literacy Association 2018), literacy coaches—even beginning literacy coaches—must demonstrate advanced knowledge and skills related to many areas of literacy as well as a strong understanding of effective professional learning (see Figure 2–1). When surveyed, 270 literacy coaches across the country affirmed that they needed a strong base of knowledge and skills to effectively work with teachers (Calo, Sturtevant, and Kopfman 2015). Literacy coaches can develop their knowledge and skills via many paths, although the completion of a sequence of coursework that leads to a master's degree in literacy is considered the "gold standard" by the International Literacy Association (Frost and Bean 2006, 2). Literacy coaches also should have a record of successful classroom teaching experience (International Literacy Association 2018), as that shows they can use their knowledge and skills to implement instruction that supports students' literacy growth.

FIGURE 2–1 *Advanced Knowledge and Skills Needed by Literacy Coaches*

AREA OF LITERACY	KNOWLEDGE	SKILLS
Foundational Knowledge	▶ Foundations of literacy and language ▶ Effective professional learning ▶ Change theory ▶ Adult learning theory	▶ Some experience planning and implementing professional learning
Curriculum and Instruction	▶ Critical components of literacy curriculum	▶ Analyze and critique literacy curricula ▶ Implement literacy curricula ▶ Design, implement, and evaluate literacy instruction aligned to the curricula
Assessment and Evaluation	▶ Screening, diagnostic, and summative tools to guide and measure student literacy learning	▶ Select assessment tools to match assessment purpose ▶ Administer, score, and use results to drive instruction ▶ Demonstrate assessment practices to teachers

(continues)

(continued)

AREA OF LITERACY	KNOWLEDGE	SKILLS
Diversity and Equity	▶ Theories, research, and concepts of diversity and equity	▶ Create learning experiences that are affirming for all students
Literacy Environment	▶ Critical components of a literacy-rich learning environment	▶ Create small groups based on need, interest, and other factors ▶ Establish routines to promote student independence ▶ Select materials that are motivating to each learner

Figure 2–1 summarizes the knowledge and skills delineated in Standards 1–6 for Reading/Literacy Specialists (International Literacy Association 2018).

Armed with this advanced knowledge, skill set, and successful teaching experience, literacy coaches will be ready to provide the appropriate support to teachers who are seeking to enhance their own knowledge and instructional practices.

What roles should the literacy coach play in a school?

Multiple studies have examined the roles and responsibilities of literacy coaches (Bean et al. 2015; Bright and Hensley 2010; Deussen et al. 2007). The results indicate that educators with the title of literacy coach generally take on one or more of the following roles: working with teachers, engaging in assessment-related tasks, managing the materials and paperwork related to interventions and curricula, and providing instruction to small groups of students. The percentage of time devoted to each role varies from coach to coach, but research indicates that it is the work with teachers that leads to growth in students' literacy learning (Bean et al. 2008; Elish-Piper and

How can coaches prioritize their time with teachers? See Section 3, pages 74–77.

L'Allier 2011). Thus, when developing job descriptions for coaches, the list of specific coaching responsibilities should give high priority to working with teachers. Figure 2–2 provides examples of teacher-focused coaching responsibilities.

FIGURE 2–2 *Teacher-Focused Coaching Responsibilities*

- Strengthen teachers' knowledge of standards-aligned, research-supported practices through a variety of professional learning opportunities such as large- and small-group workshops and book studies.

- Strengthen core instruction by working with grade-level teams and individual teachers to co-plan, model, co-teach, observe, and reflect on research-supported literacy practices.

- Support teachers in the administration and analysis of both formal and informal literacy assessments to plan needs-based instruction.

- Foster teachers' reflection about their instruction and student learning to build teachers' use of evidence-based decision making.

Principals can use the guidelines related to qualifications and job responsibilities to develop a job description that drives not only the hiring process but also the day-to-day work of literacy coaches. The guidelines can also assist with the recruitment process, helping *teachers and other literacy professionals* know if they are qualified to be a literacy coach and if they are interested in the coaching responsibilities delineated on the job description. Finally, when these guidelines are used to hire literacy coaches, *teachers* will see that coaches will be giving top priority to ongoing collaborations with teachers.

Developing Collaborative Relationships

Teachers and coaches report that trusting, collaborative relationships are critical to the coaching process (Bean et al. 2010; Vanderburg and Stephens 2010). We can begin to understand what these relationships entail by examining what teachers say they value about their coaching experiences. Vanderburg and Stephens (2010) interviewed a set of teachers from South Carolina who, with the support of literacy coaches, participated in a statewide effort to incorporate research-supported practices into their instruction. Teachers reported that the coaches were good facilitators of the study groups, which enabled them to form strong communities of learning about research-based practices, each others' teaching, and student learning. When discussing their individual work with coaches, teachers specifically named several positive coaching behaviors (see Figure 2–3).

FIGURE 2–3 *What Teachers Value in a Coaching Relationship*

Teachers value coaches who are:

- encouraging, not judgmental or evaluating,
- willing to spend time in their classrooms,
- responsive to their individual needs, and
- easily accessible while remaining true to their commitments.

These behaviors show that coaches who respect teachers avoid the perception of a power differential between coaches and teachers that can negatively impact the development of collaborative relationships (Rainville and Jones 2008).

The perception of a power differential between coaches and teachers can negatively impact the development of collaborative relationships.

Even when teachers see coaches as knowledgeable, supportive, and approachable, teachers' perceptions about the value of coaching may be influenced by the amount of time coaches spend on their various roles (Bean et al. 2010). For example, teachers viewed coaches as more valuable instructional resources in schools where coaches spent more time working with teachers and less time working with students. Teachers also viewed coaches more favorably when coaches spent less time on managerial or school-level activities.

Coaches Take on Different Stances

The nature of the conversations between teachers and coaches may also influence the development of strong collaborative relationships. Building on the ideas of Lipton and Wellman (2007), Elish-Piper and L'Allier (2014) describe three coaching discourses or stances they observed while working with literacy coaches from several large school districts in Illinois: facilitating, collaborating, and consulting (see Figure 2–4). When coaches thoroughly understand the purpose of each stance, they employ coaching language that acknowledges and shows respect for teachers' expertise while helping teachers move forward with reflective thinking, knowledge, and/or skills. In this responsive model of coaching, the teacher is in the driver's seat; the coach chooses the stance that matches the teacher's knowledge about and needs around the instructional focus. It is not unusual, therefore, for a coach to move from one coaching stance to another during a single coaching conversation. For example, if a teacher provides a cue that she wants to exchange ideas, the coach would take on the collaborative stance, but when that same teacher asks for the coach's advice about an instructional practice or next instructional steps, the coach would shift to a consulting stance. In this consulting stance, the coach continues to acknowledge the teacher's authority by offering two or three suggestions and then inviting the teacher to reflect on the options and select the option that she thinks would work best for her students. The coach's ability to shift stances strengthens the coach-teacher relationship because it builds the teacher's confidence that the coach will be able to take on several supportive roles—as a sounding board (in the facilitative stance), a thinking partner (in the collaborative stance), or a resource (in the consulting stance).

The coach's ability to shift stances strengthens the coach-teacher relationship because it builds the teacher's confidence that the coach will be able to take on several supportive roles—as a sounding board (in the facilitative stance), a thinking partner (in the collaborative stance), or a resource (in the consulting stance).

FIGURE 2–4 *Literacy Coaching Stances*

Coaching stance	Description of support	Who provides information and leads problem solving
Facilitating	The literacy coach serves as a listener and clarifier in this stance. The coach paraphrases what teachers say and asks open-ended questions. This stance is most appropriate when teachers have a good deal of knowledge about the issue and just want to have someone with whom to share ideas and discuss options.	The teacher
Collaborating	The literacy coach serves as a partner for teachers in this stance. Both the teacher and the literacy coach bring knowledge to the conversation and share in the problem-solving process. In this stance, the coach often uses inclusive language such as "we," "us," and "our" to show that he or she is working as a partner with the teacher.	The teacher and the literacy coach
Consulting	The literacy coach takes the lead in this stance when teachers are frustrated, overwhelmed, or extremely unfamiliar with the topic or issue. In this stance, the literacy coach brings most of the information to the coaching activity and takes the responsibility for leading the problem-solving process.	The literacy coach

From Elish-Piper and L'Allier (2014). Copyright © 2014 by The Guilford Press. Reprinted by permission.

In his examination of coaching stances, Ippolito (2010) identified that coaches from an urban East Coast school district exhibited two types of coaching stances: responsive and directive coaching. Ippolito defined responsive coaching as "coaching for teacher self-reflection" and directive coaching as "coaching for the implementation of particular practices" (164)—often district- and/or school-sanctioned instructional practices. Coaches reported using the directive stance when providing professional learning to large groups of teachers but stated that they were more likely to use the responsive stance when working with individual teachers. Coaches noted that it was sometimes difficult to balance responsive coaching (critical to building collaborative relationships based on teacher needs) with directive coaching (critical to addressing district priorities and initiating research-supported practices). Ippolito reported that coaches were better able to achieve this balance when they:

- shifted between stances during a single coaching session, and

- used protocols when facilitating small-group work and conferencing with individual teachers—protocols that included a dual focus on teacher needs and program goals.

Examining Specific Aspects of Coaching Conversations

To help us understand how specific aspects of coaching conversations impact collaborative relationships, Heineke (2013) built on the research around coaching stances by analyzing the transcripts of conferences between coaches and teachers. She examined who dominated the conversation, how responsive the coach was to the teacher, and who extended the ideas discussed. The results indicated that coaches contributed 65 percent of the total utterances and 80 percent of the ideas for future instructional steps. Coaches always answered questions posed by teachers but sometimes failed to acknowledge opinions or other statements made by teachers. Coaches who tend to dominate conversations and fail to respond to teachers' comments may send a message that what teachers have to say is not important—which teachers may see as a lack of respect. On the other hand, teachers were more likely to extend the conversations by sharing their own ideas or questions, one indication that the coaches and teachers had developed a collaborative relationship. Heineke concluded with ways that coaches can build successful collaborations (see Figure 2–5).

What does effective communication between a coach and teacher sound like? See Section 3, pages 48–50.

FIGURE 2–5 *Coaching Behaviors That Signify Successful Collaboration with Teachers*

Coaches who attend to the

- needs of the teachers,
- language that they use during coaching conversations,
- language that teachers use during coaching conversations, and
- commitments made to the teachers

will build a foundation for collaborative relationships that can strengthen over time.

Results from interviews and surveys suggest that a trusting, collaborative relationship lays the foundation for intentional coaching work. However, we do not know the extent to which the coach-teacher relationship impacts changes in teacher practice and/or student learning. This is definitely an area needing further research.

Coaching: An Essential Tool for School Change

Coaches provide job-embedded professional development to teachers to improve teacher practice and increase student learning. Researchers have examined the impact of coaching in both of these areas, and an overview of several of these studies is presented in Figure 2–6. Results indicate that coaching is effective in helping teachers focus on specific elements of a school- or district-wide initiative. Coaching has also been found to help teachers provide more explicit instruction about aspects of literacy such as comprehension strategies and instruction-related features of the classroom environment. In addition, coaching has been found to contribute to student learning for all students. More specifically, the results of some studies have shown a positive impact of coaching on English Language Learners (ELLs) and on students reading below benchmark.

FIGURE 2–6 *Examples of Studies on the Effect of Coaching on Teacher Practice and Student Learning*

COACHING PROGRAM	TEACHER PRACTICE	STUDENT LEARNING
Minnesota Reading Project ▶ Twenty-four schools ▶ 1.5 coaches per school ▶ Coaches expected to spend 80% of time working with teachers (Taylor and Peterson 2006; Taylor et al. 2007)	Increase in instructional time over a three-year period: Time spent on higher-order talk increased from ▶ 17% to 21%—grade 2 ▶ 22% to 26% —grade 3. Time spent on writing instruction increased from ▶ 17% to 21%—grade 2 ▶ 22% to 26%—grade 3. Time spent teaching comprehension strategies increased from ▶ 4% to 16%—grade 2 ▶ 11% to 18%—grade 3.	This study did not examine student learning.
Prekindergarten language and literacy programs compared: ▶ teachers who received university coursework and coaching, ▶ teachers who received university coursework only, and ▶ teachers who received neither. (Neuman and Cunningham 2009; Neuman and Wright 2010)	Coached teachers scored higher on measures of: ▶ literacy environment design (2009, 2010), ▶ supports for learning (2009), and ▶ teaching strategies (2009).	This study did not examine student learning.

(continues)

(continued)

COACHING PROGRAM	TEACHER PRACTICE	STUDENT LEARNING
Content-Focused Coaching (CFC) Compared teachers who: ► received CFC ► received general coaching. (Matsumura et al. 2010, 2013)	► Higher-quality text discussion practices occurred with teachers receiving CFC. ► More participation in coaching was seen in CFC teachers.	The following changes were documented in CFC schools: ► more interactive and rigorous discussions, ► higher reading achievement, and ► narrowed achievement gap between ELLs and non-ELLs.
South Carolina Reading Initiative (SCRI) Teachers received: ► small-group professional learning and ► individual coaching. (Stephens et al. 2011)	Teachers became more consistent with beliefs and practices of the SCRI.	This study did not examine student learning.
Reading First compared: ► teachers who received professional development and coaching, ► teachers who received professional development only, and ► teachers who received neither. (Carlisle and Berebitsky 2011)	Teachers who received professional development and coaching showed increased implementation of Reading First components.	Greater improvement in word decoding seen in students in classes where coaching took place.

COACHING PROGRAM	TEACHER PRACTICE	STUDENT LEARNING
Support for Improvement of Practices Through Intensive Coaching (SIPIC) compared teachers who: ▶ received two-day workshop plus SIPIC and ▶ received two-day workshop. (Sailors and Price 2015)	▶ SIPIC teachers engaged in more comprehension strategy instruction. ▶ SIPIC teachers gave better explanations of comprehension strategies to students.	▶ Students whose teachers received SIPIC had greater gains on standardized reading assessments. ▶ Greatest improvement in SIPIC settings was made by students classified as below-grade level.

In some of the studies referenced in Figure 2–6, coaching was a component of a school-wide reform effort such as Reading First (Carlisle and Berebitsky 2011) or the Minnesota Reading Project (Taylor and Peterson 2006; Taylor et al. 2007). Let's examine the results on student learning of the Literacy Collaborative, another school-wide reform initiative that included a coaching component. The Literacy Collaborative had the goal of improving student literacy learning through the use of a comprehensive literacy framework (i.e., a framework that included reading, writing, and language). Coaches in the Literacy Collaborative received a year of professional development about the literacy framework and coaching before beginning to work with teachers. After receiving this training, coaches taught half time and provided professional development about the literacy framework to individual teachers during the other half of their day. During the first year of implementation, teachers also completed a forty-hour workshop about the literacy framework—workshops that were facilitated by the coaches. Biancarosa, Bryk, and Dexter (2010) examined the four-year learning pattern of K–2 students taught in seventeen Literacy Collaborative Schools across eight states. The first year, when coaches were being trained and the teachers were following their schools' regular curricula, served as a baseline year. During this year, the average growth rate was 1.02. This growth was then compared with the growth that students made when the teacher workshop and coaching components of the Literacy Collaborative were in place. In each subsequent year, average student learning improved over the baseline year and over the previous year (see Figure 2–7).

FIGURE 2–7 *The Effect of the Literacy Collaborative on Student Learning*

YEAR	COMPARED TO YEAR 1 BASELINE GROWTH RATE OF 1.02%
2	16% increase in learning
3	28% increase in learning
4	32% increase in learning

As coaching was considered "the cornerstone" of the Literacy Collaborative (Atteberry and Bryk 2011, 357), these results certainly support the use of literacy coaching as a component of a well-designed school-wide literacy initiative.

Further support for coaching comes from Kraft, Blazar, and Hogan (2018) who combined the results of sixty studies focused on professional development. All programs in the studies included the following:

- a coaching component and

- a measure of teacher practice, usually a structured observational tool, and/or a measure of student achievement as measured by a standardized assessment.

Results indicated that these professional development efforts had a medium positive effect (0.49) on teacher practice; this change in teacher practice is larger than the instructional differences between novice and veteran teachers! In addition, these programs had a small positive effect (0.18) on student achievement; this change in student achievement was similar to the difference between the student achievement of first-year teachers and the student achievement of teachers who have taught for five to ten years! Once again, we see that positive outcomes result when coaches provide job-embedded professional development to teachers within the scope of systematic professional development efforts.

> *Positive outcomes result when coaches provide job-embedded professional development to teachers within the scope of systematic professional development efforts.*

Which Coaching Activities Impact Instruction?

As discussed earlier, coaches are often expected to complete a wide variety of tasks. In their study of coaching in grades K–3 in 116 high-poverty schools, Walpole et al. (2010) used observation protocols to examine which coaching activities were related to specific teacher practices. The results indicated that three coaching factors (i.e., constructive collaboration, coaching for differentiation, and leadership support for coaching) predicted one or more instructional factors (i.e., small-group work, effective reading instruction, and management), but the results differed by grade level as shown in Figure 2–8.

FIGURE 2–8 *Coaching Factors Predictive of Instructional Factors at Specific Grade Levels*

Coaching Factor/ Instructional Factor (Results from Walpole et al. 2010)	Collaboration (constructive interactions between coach and teachers at group and individual levels; effective interactions with reluctant teachers)	Coaching for Differentiation (interpretation of assessment data, grouping, co-planning)	Leadership Support for Coaching (coach and principal collaborate constructively; principal supports planning for small-group instruction; principal participates in professional learning)
Small-group work (adequately planned, goal stated to students, all students engaged, good pacing and time management)	Third grade		Kindergarten, first and second grades

(continues)

(continued)

Coaching Factor/ Instructional Factor	Collaboration	Coaching for Differentiation	Leadership Support for Coaching
Effective reading instruction (including research-based practices in phonological awareness, fluency, vocabulary, comprehension; scaffolded teacher feedback; adjusting lesson to student needs)	Third grade	First grade	
Management (clear system for group work, students understand procedures; optimal student engagement, quick transitions)	Third grade		

Which Coaching Activities Impact Student Growth?

Elish-Piper and L'Allier (2011) wanted to find out which coaching activities would be most important for increasing student achievement. In their study of twelve literacy coaches serving 121 teachers in a high-poverty school district, four coaching activities were found to be significant predictors of student achievement (see Figure 2–9). As was the case with the study by Walpole et al. (2010), there were differences in predictors across grade levels.

FIGURE 2–9 *Coaching Activities Predictive of Student Literacy Growth*

COACHING ACTIVITIES	KINDERGARTEN	FIRST GRADE	SECOND GRADE
Conferencing	X	Approached significance	X
Modeling			X
Observing			X
Assessing related activities		X	X

It is important to note that two or more of these four coaching activities were the core coaching activities delineated in the studies cited previously in this section. Thus, principals, coaches, and teachers should all understand why coaches prioritize conferencing, modeling, observation, and assessment-related activities when developing their weekly schedules.

Why might these four coaching activities lead to improved student learning?

For examples of how these coaching activities fit into a coaching cycle, see Section 3, pages 54–71.

Conferencing

Conferencing between coaches and teachers generally occurs before and after a lesson that the coach has modeled, the coach and teacher have co-taught, or the teacher has implemented. The pre-teaching conferences provide teachers opportunities to co-plan lessons that are aligned with learning standards, use research-supported strategies, and incorporate the gradual release of responsibility model (McVee et al. 2019; Pearson and Gallagher 1983). The post-teaching conferences provide opportunities for teachers to reflect on instructional practices and on the student learning that resulted from those practices. During these conversations, the coach uses observational data and open-ended questions to deepen the teacher's reflections. This reflective behavior enables teachers to make evidence-based decisions about future instruction, groupings, and assessment—decisions that foster student growth in literacy.

Modeling for Teachers

Teachers may not feel confident about their ability to implement some of the new research-supported instructional practices they are learning. This lack of confidence may deter some teachers from implementing practices that could strengthen student learning. Coaches can build teacher confidence and foster the use of new practices by modeling those practices in the teachers' classrooms so that teachers can see how those practices work with their own students.

Observations of Teachers

Teachers are often so immersed in their teaching that they have difficulty reflecting in-the-moment on lesson specifics. As observers, coaches can focus on specific aspects of the instruction (e.g., teacher questioning, pacing, student time on task, depth of student responses) that may strengthen teacher practice, student engagement, and/or student learning.

Assessment-Related Activities

Teachers often need the support of a coach with many aspects of assessment including the administration and scoring of assessments, the use of informal assessments, and the use of assessment results to drive instruction. Teachers must become proficient in these assessment-related activities to create instruction aligned with expected student outcomes and to determine when those outcomes have been achieved.

In Section 3, Erin describes ways that coaches and teachers can consistently incorporate conferencing, modeling, observation, and the use of appropriate assessments in their work and how these collaborations have resulted in enhanced teacher practice as well as improved student literacy learning.

Principals as Partners

Research has provided an understanding of how some of the ways administrators view themselves supporting literacy coaching and how these supportive actions may influence teacher participation in coaching activities. In addition, researchers have examined how coaches view the role that administrators play in the coaching program.

Studies of successful schools and successful school reform efforts have found that principal leadership is an essential component of positive outcomes (Bryk et al. 2010; Camburn, Rowan, and Taylor 2003; Supovitz, Sirinides, and May 2010). More specifically, principal leadership influences the effectiveness of teacher leaders, including literacy coaches (Carlisle and Berebitsky 2011; Mangin 2007). How administrators provide support to these teacher leaders appears to be a critical aspect of their leadership.

A study by Matsumura et al. (2009) provides us with more specific details about the nature of administrative support. Matsumura and her colleagues examined the effects of a coaching program known as Content-Focused Coaching (CFC). As coaches received a year of professional learning about coaching teachers to enhance text discussions using the Questioning the Author approach (Beck and McKeown 2006), they facilitated grade-level meetings and coached individual teachers to use that approach. Individual coaching included modeling, co-planning lessons, co-teaching, and observation of the teacher's lessons. Structured interviews with principals as well as data about teacher participation in the various coaching activities enabled the researchers to examine specific ways that principals supported coaches and fostered teacher participation. The qualitative analysis of the principal interviews revealed three dimensions of principal support. Moreover, these principal behaviors were positively associated with teacher participation in specific coaching activities critical to the CFC program (see Figure 2–10).

FIGURE 2–10 *The Relationship Between Principal Support of the Coaching Program and Teacher Participation in Coaching Activities*

Principal Support	HIGHER TEACHER PARTICIPATION	
	Grade-Level Meetings	Coach Observation of Teacher Instruction
Treated the coach as a valued professional	X	X
Publicly endorsed the coach as a source of literacy expertise to teachers		X
Actively participated in the Content-Focused Coaching program (e.g., participated in professional learning sessions with their coaches, participated in large-group training led by the coach; attended team meetings facilitated by coach)	X	X

An additional finding (Matsumura et al. 2009) was that principals in schools with higher teacher participation attended the CFC training sessions for principals and gave coaches autonomy over their schedules. Principal attendance at the training sessions may have provided them with a deep understanding of CFC so that they could knowledgeably endorse the program and have confidence in the coaches' ability to develop their own schedules. In contrast, the results of a study by Camburn, Kimball, and Lowenhaupt (2008) indicated that there was less teacher participation in coaching activities when principals set the schedule or tasks for coaches.

Researchers have also examined how coaches view the role of administrators (Bean et al. 2015; Calo, Sturtevant, and Kopfman 2015; Matsumura et al. 2009). Matsumura and her colleagues

(2009) provided specific examples of the supportive behaviors cited by coaches when interviewed about the implementation of the CFC program (see Figure 2–11).

FIGURE 2–11 *How Coaches Felt Supported by Their Principals*

PRINCIPAL BEHAVIORS REPORTED BY COACHES	BECAUSE OF THIS BEHAVIOR, COACHES THOUGHT TEACHERS WOULD BE MORE LIKELY TO . . .
Principals explicitly explained or endorsed the coaching program.	Engage in the program because teachers typically align their goals and actions with the priorities of their principals.
Principals identified coaches as resources.	Seek out the coaches' help with problems that arise when implementing the text discussion lessons.
Principals encouraged teachers to work with coaches.	Participate in the grade-level meetings and the individual coaching sessions.
Principals observed coaching activities such as the modeling of lessons.	Value these coaching activities and to appreciate the coaches' openness for observation.

On a more personal basis, coaches felt supported because the principal specifically told them that their work with teachers was valued. Because there is typically only one coach in each building, coaches can feel isolated; positive comments from principals encourage them to move forward with their work.

Even in studies where coaches reported that their administrators were supportive, they often voiced the need for even more support (Calo et al. 2015; Mangin 2007). Coaches wanted their principals to collaborate in the development of clearly defined goals for the program and revision of the coach's job description, to have regularly scheduled coach-principal meetings, and to more strongly encourage teachers to work with them.

> For examples of principal communications that define, clarify, and support the coaching program, see Section 3, pages 80–83.

There is strong evidence from research that coaches:

- think administrative support is powerful,

- desire administrative support, and

- often don't feel supported by administrators.

In fact, in a national survey of more than 2,500 reading professionals (Bean et al. 2015), only one-third of the coaches felt supported by their administrator "to a great extent" (93). Clearly, this
is an area for improvement! Examples of ways coaches and administrators build collaborative, supporting relationships are described
in Section 3.

Coaches as Literacy Leaders

We have seen how coaches spend time working with individual
teachers to strengthen instructional practices and improve student
literacy. In numerous studies, coaches also report that they serve
as literacy leaders in a variety of other ways (Bean et al. 2008,
2015; Bean and Lillenstein 2012; Bright and Hensley 2010; Calo,
Sturtevant, and Kopfman 2015; Elish-Piper and L'Allier 2010). The
following summary of these leadership activities can be separated
into two categories: leadership at the teacher level and leadership
at the school and/or district level.

Leadership at the Teacher Level

Providing Large-Group Professional Development. Coaches
report that they are often responsible for planning and delivering
professional development to large groups of teachers—such as all
teachers responsible for literacy instruction or all K–3 teachers.
These large-group presentations help build a shared understanding
of the content and are most effective when they establish the foundation for subsequent ongoing coaching at the small-group and/or
individual level.

Facilitating Grade-Level or Small-Group Meetings. These meetings offer opportunities to:

- provide professional learning around an area of teacher or
  student need,

- analyze formal and informal assessment results,

- co-plan data-driven instruction and reflect on the implementation of that instruction, and

- provide additional support to individual teachers through modeling, co-teaching, and observation.

Facilitating Book Studies. About 45 percent of the coaches surveyed by Calo, Sturtevant, and Kopfman (2015) reported that they facilitated book studies. Book studies can help teachers learn about, implement, and reflect on research-based strategies for improving student literacy when:

- Books are carefully chosen to meet the needs and interests of the teachers and are aligned with learning standards and research-supported practices.

- Teachers read the designated pages before each session.

- Coaches use protocols to ensure the most efficient use of the book study sessions.

Developing Teacher Leaders. Over time, coaches become aware of teachers who show strengths in literacy knowledge, instruction, and reflection. These teachers are prime candidates to become teacher leaders. Developing teacher leaders is one way to build leadership capacity across the building. Coaches can support the development of teacher leaders by:

For real-life examples of how coaches develop teacher leaders, see Section 3, pages 78–80.

- encouraging them to allow other teachers to observe their instruction and talking with those teachers about the decision making involved when planning instruction,

- asking them to co-present at a professional development session and helping them prepare their portion of the presentation, and

- supporting them in the facilitation of grade-level meetings so that grade-level teams can function effectively even when the coach is not in attendance.

Leadership at the School and/or District Level

Serving on the Building Leadership Team. Coaches who serve on the building leadership teams are able to provide input into school-wide decisions such as the focus of the school improvement plan and the yearlong plan for professional development. They are able to use their knowledge about program evaluation to help select and determine the effectiveness of new curricula. In addition, they make recommendations about organizational changes that would support teachers as they strive to enact the action steps of the school improvement plan or implement new instructional practices. One organizational change that coaches frequently recommend is to build a school-wide schedule that provides common planning time for each grade level—so each grade-level team can collaborate with the coach to address common instructional challenges.

> *Coaches frequently recommend building a school-wide schedule that provides common planning time for each grade level.*

Analyzing School-wide Data. Seventy-two percent of the coaches surveyed by Calo, Sturtevant, and Kopfman (2015) reported that they led or participated in the analysis of school-wide data, including literacy data. When coaches analyze school-wide literacy data, they are assisting the leadership team in determining areas that are challenging for many students in the school as well areas that are problematic at specific grade levels or for specific groups of students. The results help coaches determine needs for large-group and small-group coaching.

Collaborating with Other Specialists. Most schools employ multiple specialists. In the schools where we work, these specialists typically include a literacy coach, a reading specialist or interventionist who works with small groups of students, and one or more special education professionals. Some schools are fortunate to also have math and technology coaches. Literacy coaches find it important to meet with the other specialists on a regular basis to ensure that they are coordinating their efforts to support teachers and students. This coordination is critical because teachers may become overwhelmed if they are expected to work and conference with several different people during the same time period.

Serving on the District Curriculum Committee. Ninety-three percent of the coaches surveyed by Calo, Sturtevant, and Kopfman (2015) reported that they were literacy leaders at the school level; 66 percent also reported leadership responsibilities at the district level. These coaches specified that they were members of district curriculum teams and/or participated in district professional development. Because of their district-level involvement, coaches were able to help teachers understand the connections between the literacy program at the school level and the literacy endeavors at the district level.

A Gentle Reminder: The Majority of Coaches' Time Should Be Spent Working Directly with Teachers

Although almost all coaches report that their role includes various leadership responsibilities, research results indicate that time working directly with teachers is the key to improving teacher practice and student learning. In studies that found changes in practice and achievement, coaches spent their time providing professional development to large groups and grade-level teams as well as providing individual coaching through conferencing, co-planning, co-teaching, and observing (for example, Bean et al. 2008; Biancarosa, Bryk, and Dexter 2010; Elish-Piper and L'Allier 2011; Matsumura et al. 2010, 2013). In Section 3, Erin shares some ways that coaches can develop and maintain schedules that allocate the majority of their time to working with teachers.

Coaches spent their time providing professional development to large groups and grade-level teams as well as providing individual coaching through conferencing, co-planning, co-teaching, and observing.

Invitation for Further Research

To date, research has given us a picture of the myriad roles and responsibilities of literacy coaches. Researchers have also examined the discourse that coaches and teachers use when working together and the importance of administrator support for coaching. Results of other studies have indicated a positive impact of coaching on enhancing teacher practice and increasing student literacy growth.

Research in the following areas would help administrators, coaches, and teachers gain more understanding about how to design an effective coaching program:

- Principals, when considering their staffing resources, have often asked us if their coaches could work half-time with students to provide needed interventions and half-time with teachers. Aside from the coaches in the Literacy Collaborative (Atteberry and Bryk 2011), most of the research has focused on full-time coaches. By examining the impact of a half-time coaching model on teacher practice and student growth, researchers could help principals make informed decisions about an effective coaching model.

- Principals and coaches have also asked, "How many teachers should a coach be expected to work with at any one time?" Some principals would like their coaches to work with every teacher in some manner throughout the year—which coaches find very difficult to achieve, especially in larger schools. Research by Yoon and her colleagues (2007) and Desimone (2009) suggests that teacher change in one area of practice requires fourteen to twenty hours of professional learning—which could include summer and school-year workshops, grade-level coaching, and individual coaching. Currently, the number of teachers with whom coaches work varies widely from study to study (Bean et al. 2010; Elish-Piper and L'Allier 2011). Future studies could provide principals and coaches a research-supported recommendation about this important question.

- Researchers (Biancarosa, Bryk, and Dexter 2010; Elish-Piper and L'Allier 2011; Marsh et al. 2008) have wondered how to define a replicable model of coaching efficacy. Additional understanding about the critical components would foster smooth beginnings of new coaching programs and would help coaches determine what types of professional learning could further strengthen their coaching knowledge, skills, and dispositions.

In Section 3, Erin shares how coaches, teachers, and principals have worked together to design and implement research-supported coaching programs that address the needs of their students.

SECTION **3**

BUT ● THAT

Coaching Strategies to Enhance Teacher Practice and Improve Student Learning

ERIN BROWN

*E*very school is an ecosystem of teachers, coaches, and the principal who are dependent on one another for success. In a recent coaching institute, a teacher who was new to coaching exclaimed, "Every teacher deserves a coach!" When a school provides coaching for teachers, that support can nourish the ecosystem like fresh rain soaking soil. As Susan discussed in Section 2, providing educators with the opportunity to think through instructional decisions with a partner improves outcomes for students. Collaborative coaching also brings great joy to teachers. Teaching can be isolating. Coaching can be a replenishing gift.

Positive Curiosity Leads to Relationships and Impact

Coaching isn't about fixing. It's filled with respect for the art of what happens with students in a school every day. A coach's appreciation of a teacher's strengths allows for real learning to happen during their conversations. At its most basic, coaching provides a new perspective on student learning for teachers. This fresh perspective is unique in a field where much of our work is done isolated from other adults. Unless in a teaming or co-teaching situation, we rarely work side by side with both students *and* other colleagues. This can sometimes make coaching feel uncomfortable to teachers when it's new in a school. Teachers who have only been able to collaborate with each other in meetings can feel unprepared to work closely with someone else in their classrooms. They sometimes fear that the coach will judge them and won't understand the decisions they make.

Coaching isn't about fixing.

45

So, when coaches start with an innate fascination with what teachers and students already do, it sets the stage for what coaches and teachers can learn and do together. A coach's respectful stance and genuine interest support a teacher's comfort level and willingness to collaborate. Teachers value a coach when they see that the coaching relationship is designed to support their thinking, enhance the decisions they make, and boost their results with students.

Teachers who have only been able to collaborate with each other in meetings can feel unprepared to work closely with someone else in their classrooms. They sometimes fear that the coach will judge them and won't understand the decisions they make.

A challenge exists in the urgency to develop a positive collaborative relationship early and quickly. One pitfall is the idea that coaches and teachers need to spend long stretches of time getting to know each other's style, routines, and preferences. As a new literacy coach, I remember the temptation to think that if I don't have a deep relationship with each colleague, my service won't be effective because they won't trust what I have to offer. Luckily, I quickly learned that collaborative relationships are strengthened *during* the work done side by side with students.

Communication That Clarifies and Creates Commitment

As in all healthy relationships, literacy coaches and teachers share responsibility in establishing and maintaining the coaching relationship. Figure 3–1 outlines the commitment and communication priorities that set a coaching relationship up for success. Working intentionally as colleagues provides clarity and confidence that the goals set together will have the intended outcomes on improved student learning. As you read the coach and teacher conversation in Figure 3–2, you will see how their language illustrates a strong commitment to their collaborative work.

Literacy coaches and teachers share responsibility in establishing and maintaining the coaching relationship.

FIGURE 3–1 *Coaching Commitment and Communication*

Coach-to-teacher commitments include:

- ▶ being responsive to the teacher's ideas and student needs
- ▶ providing research-supported information and practices
- ▶ following through on action items
- ▶ arriving on time to scheduled sessions and conversations
- ▶ avoiding rescheduling (outside of emergencies)
- ▶ staying focused and engaged the full time together.

Coach communication is effective when it:

- ▶ is encouraging and not judgmental or evaluative
- ▶ includes regular pausing and paraphrasing to support teacher metacognition
- ▶ shifts between facilitating, collaborating, and consulting stances as needed
- ▶ supports teacher reflection, with questions and key ideas prepared ahead of time
- ▶ focuses mainly on evidence and student learning.

← **Communication** →

Commitment

Commitment

Teacher communication is effective when it:

- ▶ is positive, open, and treated like any other collaborative exchange of ideas with a colleague
- ▶ honestly identifies current needs as they change across time
- ▶ is reflective, with questions and thoughts considered ahead of time
- ▶ focuses mainly on evidence and student learning.

Teacher-to-coach commitments include:

- ▶ maintaining student learning as the main goal
- ▶ being willing to try research-supported practices
- ▶ following through on action items
- ▶ honoring agreed-upon times together
- ▶ avoiding rescheduling (outside of emergencies)
- ▶ staying focused and engaged the full time together.

FIGURE 3–2 *An Effective Coaching Conversation*

COACHING CONVERSATION	COMMUNICATION AND COMMITMENT EXAMPLES
Coach: "Hi again, Anita! I'm glad we are able to talk so soon after the writing lesson today. Thank you for meeting with me so we can debrief and look ahead."	Positive, open communication
Teacher: "Thank you, too, Liz. I think the lesson went well today. The students seemed really engaged and I was pleasantly surprised that so many of them were able to get a solid start on their brochures."	Focusing mainly on evidence and student learning
Coach: "Absolutely! So, when we co-planned Wednesday, you asked me to observe specifically for two different things: student engagement during the independent writing time and your language during the lesson. You wanted to know how many times you used the key terms and phrases like heading, organizational structure, and writer's purpose as you modeled different structures for the example brochure during the lesson. When we co-planned for this lesson, we made this T-chart together with these two areas of focus: student engagement and teacher use of terms. I was able to jot many examples and evidence in both columns."	Being responsive to teacher's ideas
Teacher: "Great! I can't wait to hear the details. Thanks for providing another set of eyes . . . and ears!"	Positive and open
Coach: "My pleasure! OK, so first you were hoping to learn how often you repeated the specific informational text vocabulary you selected throughout your lesson. Your goal was to provide repetition so your students would have multiple exposures to the important terms. I tallied that you said heading six times, organizational structure eight times, table two times, and writer's purpose six times. And you added a sentence strip with a quick definition of heading and organizational structure to provide a visual for these two terms."	Focusing mainly on evidence and student learning

Coach: "It was effective when you pointed at these terms when you said them because the students' eyes went right to the words consistently . . . and you pointed every time you said either of these words—I was watching! What made you decide to create these sentence strips for the lesson today?"	Supporting teacher reflection, with questions and key ideas prepared ahead of time
Teacher: "Oh, I was thinking after we met and co-planned how I really want kids to feel comfortable using these terms, but that I have some students who might need extra support. I decided to just add these two terms and a quick definition because I knew I would have the students share out with a small group at the end. I planned to ask the students to use the terms when they explained what they tried in their writing, so I wanted to have the sentence strips ready and model the use of the language right from the beginning of the lesson."	Maintaining student learning as the main goal Honestly identifying current needs as they change across time
Coach: "So, you considered the end goal for the lesson and worked backward so your students would hear you model using some tools that could support their talk about their writing . . ."	Pausing and paraphrasing
Teacher: "Yes, and I'm really glad I chose to be so repetitive with it . . . I didn't know I said the words and pointed out that many times, but I guess that makes sense since I try to say the lesson target several times in natural ways during a writing lesson."	Being reflective
Coach: "Well, it is clear that your choices supported students because if we look here on this side of the chart, I took notes on student engagement and one way I took notes here was by writing down little quotes of what students were saying. At the end I tallied how many times I heard students use the terms—both during the lesson and as I sat with one group for the sharing time. You'll see here that . . . "	Focusing mainly on evidence and student learning

Invitational coaching language opens up our thinking. The following is a representative list of coaching stems that have been generated by groups of literacy coaches. What phrases would you add to this list?

"Tell me more about . . ."

"What does that look like in your classroom?" or "How might that look in your classroom?"

"Have you considered . . ."

"I wonder . . ."

"The way you (did something) was impactful because . . ."

"What decisions were you making instructionally as you taught this lesson?"

"What might have contributed to the success that your students had? What might have contributed to the difficulties that some of your students had?"

"What may I do to support you?"

Responsive Coaching in Individual and Small- and Large-Group Settings

We read in Section 2 that research suggests it takes fourteen to twenty hours of professional learning to change instructional practice in a specific area. This is another reason why "random acts of coaching" do not have an impact on student achievement. Without a plan, it would be hard to meet this fourteen- to twenty-hour threshold and ensure that learning will be sustained. But one-on-one coaching isn't the only mode of learning for teachers. If we only relied on individual coaching for professional learning, it would take much longer to support all teachers in a school to meet their instructional goals. In contrast, effective coaches use intentional planning and many different formats of learning and collaboration to achieve deep knowledge in a practice we want to introduce, strengthen, or change.

Research suggests it takes fourteen to twenty hours of professional learning to change instructional practice in a specific area.

FIGURE 3–3 *A Nested Professional Learning Model*

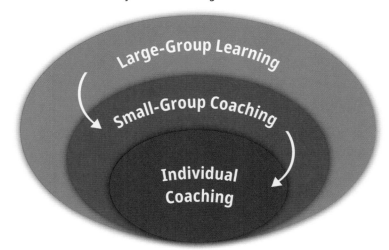

A nested approach to professional learning (Figure 3–3) shows how individual coaching can be an outgrowth of whole-school learning. For each of these three modes of learning, the coach and the teacher both have important roles.

The coach is often the:

- presenter or co-presenter for large-group professional learning,
- facilitator for small-group coaching, and
- thinking partner at the individual coaching level.

The teacher is often the:

- active participant during large-group professional learning,
- collaborator and contributor when participating in small-group coaching, and
- collaborator and reflector when participating in individual coaching.

Let's look at how a leadership team comprised of Kaitlyn, the coach, Ovetta, the principal, and a set of teacher leaders used the nested approach to address the school-wide goal of using more flexible small-group instruction. To begin to address this goal, the team planned a semester-long learning trajectory that started with some large-group professional learning sessions. See Figure 3–4.

FIGURE 3–4 *Large-Group Professional Learning*

The leadership team co-planned several staff meetings that focused on needs-based small-group teaching. During these sessions, Kaitlyn provided explicit guidelines and examples of how to:

- examine their observation and assessment data,
- identify specific student needs,
- design lessons and select materials to meet the identified student needs, and
- reflect on lessons taught and plan future small-group lessons based on observation and formative assessment.

Now that teachers had begun to understand the fundamentals of data-driven small group instruction, they were ready to apply that learning more specifically. To facilitate this move, Kaitlyn turned to small-group coaching, scheduling weekly meetings with a small group of lower elementary teachers. See Figure 3–5.

FIGURE 3–5 *Small-Group Coaching*

Focus: To drill deeper into student phonics needs and create small-group instruction based on those needs.

Activities:

- Kaitlyn worked with the teachers to co-plan a series of lessons for each small group by reflecting on data that showed the specific needs of groups of students.

- After teachers implemented the lessons, Kaitlyn facilitated teacher reflection about the lessons in terms of student learning and continuing questions. Teachers shared that students could use the targeted phonics skills during small-group lessons, but weren't sure students were applying the skills in real reading.

- Kaitlyn designed a possible lesson plan template that teachers could use for any phonics-based small-group lesson that included a section about how teachers could determine if their students were applying the phonics skills during their supported independent reading.

While these small-group coaching sessions were happening, two teachers decided they would benefit from working with Kaitlyn on an individual basis. See Figure 3–6.

FIGURE 3–6 *Individual Coaching*

Kaitlyn modeled several small-group lessons to:

- demonstrate how to use the lesson plan template with a variety of small groups, and

- discuss her in-the-moment decision making during the lessons.

After modeling, Kaitlyn observed and provided support as each teacher taught small-group lessons using the lesson plan template.

As Kaitlyn reflected on the work thus far, she knew that a valuable next step would be for the other teachers to observe each of these teachers in action. See Figure 3–7.

FIGURE 3–7 *Small-Group Coaching Observation*

- During their common meeting time, the lower elementary teachers observed each of the two teachers teach a small-group lesson to their students.

- Following the lessons, Kaitlyn facilitated a discussion during which:

  - the two teachers shared how they planned their lessons and reflected on how the lesson plan template supported their instruction and their students' learning, and

  - Kaitlyn used open-ended questions and paraphrasing to encourage the other teachers to ask questions and offer additional reflections.

Across these structures, Kaitlyn consistently chose approaches to support the most efficient use of her time and to build collaboration among teachers. Most importantly, the result was student growth. As they collected observation notes and student assessment data, the literacy leadership team noticed an immediate increase in the students' foundational skills knowledge! So many educators were responsible for the outcomes of this process—the principal, the coach, and the teachers—and each played a role in the collective success. See Figure 3–8.

FIGURE 3–8 *Decision Making About the Nested Model*

BEGIN WITH . . .	IF . . .
Large-Group Professional Learning	There is a need for shared understanding/learning by a large group of teachers.
Small-Group Coaching	There are common needs or goals within specific grade levels or other small teams of teachers.
Individual Coaching	Some teachers are requesting support in unique areas of literacy instruction.

Coaching Cycles to Enhance Teacher Practice and Student Learning

A coaching cycle is an articulated plan for the work that happens between a teacher and a coach, based on a specific goal. Successful coaching cycles are built on the belief that the person being coached is capable of accomplishing the goals they have set.

■ The coach's role in a cycle is to support and advance the teaching decisions made to achieve a goal in the shortest time possible.

■ The teacher's role in a cycle is to invite someone into their thinking so they can revise and enhance what they know.

As we begin a coaching cycle, we can ask the centering question that my colleague and mathematics coaching expert, Kristin, recently asked in a coaching meeting: "What can we do together that only can be done *because* we are working together?" Isn't that a grounding question? To me, it's a reminder of the acceleration and growth that comes from teaching side by side with someone when hyper-focused on a common purpose. Thinking about what we can accomplish together that we could not accomplish alone drives teachers to choose ambitious goals. Teachers know they won't be left struggling to figure out how to achieve those goals on their own.

Coaching Cycles Are Predictable Yet Flexible

There is no magic to a coaching cycle. The format is meant to be simple and predictable, but flexible enough to meet the needs of the teacher.

As we learned in Section 2, the coaching activities that were found to be most important for increasing student achievement were conferencing (including co-planning as one type of conference), modeling, observing, and assessment-related activities. In the model in Figure 3–9, *conferencing* is seen in the circle surrounding all the other coaching activities, because it is the common activity that glues a coaching cycle together.

Successful coaching cycles are built on the belief that the person being coached is capable of accomplishing the goals they have set.

Let's look more closely at the components of a typical coaching cycle.

- ■ The first step in most coaching cycles is *goal setting*. The coach and teacher(s) come together to discuss the specific work they might do together to support students. In this conference, they define a data-informed student learning goal.

- ■ After determining a specific and measurable goal for their collaboration, the coach and teacher(s) begin to *co-plan* the first lessons and other activities they will use to work toward the goal. While *co-planning*, they often decide to follow the gradual release of responsibility approach (McVee et al. 2019) where the coach will begin with *modeling* a specific instructional practice, later will move to *co-teaching* with the teacher, and then will switch to *observing* and providing feedback as the teacher takes on the instruction.

■ The decisions made during the co-planning phase are fluid and may be revised throughout the *implementation* phase of a coaching cycle as the coach and teacher watch students and reflect together. Modeling, co-teaching, and observing are chosen intentionally throughout a coaching cycle depending on what is needed to meet a particular goal. Many factors come into play when deciding which coaching activities will best meet needs in a coaching cycle, including how familiar the coach and teacher are with each other's teaching, the depth of the instructional goal, and the predicted length of the coaching cycle.

■ Between each teaching episode, the coach and teacher *conference* to reflect, revise, and co-plan next instructional steps. During these conferences, the coach and teacher use *observation and informal assessments* to revise the next steps needed to achieve the goal.

■ As you can see, conversations become the center of any coaching cycle. Once coaches and teachers start teaching together, their conversations are usually filled with honest reflection in light of the initial goal. And they don't have to wait until the end of a planned coaching cycle to *revisit their goal*! Hopefully the goal is woven into all of their conferences. When comparing the goal with what they are noticing through intentional observations of students' learning, they determine which students have achieved the goal or a part of the goal at any point in the cycle and what instructional steps to take with those who are still working toward the goal. Sometimes it's the real work of teaching side-by-side that helps colleagues realize that a goal might need to be refined to better meet key learning standards or research-supported literacy practices. Conferencing regularly helps teachers and coaches calibrate their decisions as they move toward their shared goal.

Sometimes it's the real work of teaching side-by-side that helps colleagues realize that a goal might need to be refined to better meet key learning standards or research-supported literacy practices.

FIGURE 3–9 *The Coaching Cycle*

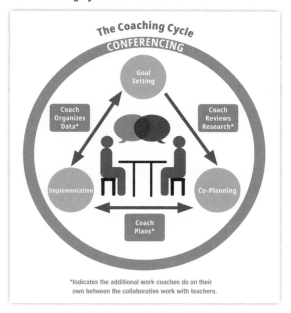

It's easy for service-oriented, generous coaches to overschedule themselves by participating in too many coaching cycles simultaneously, leaving little time during the workday to personally prepare for coaching. Coaching cycles are often about employing new practices or modifying structures in a classroom. Although the coach may have initial understanding of the practices needed to meet a coaching cycle goal, it takes time to read or revisit related literacy research and thoroughly prepare for the instructional activities. Figure 3–9 makes visible this often invisible planning work a coach does to be organized and ready for each step in a coaching cycle.

1. **Reviewing Research.** Right after a specific goal is set with a teacher or group, a coach usually spends time refreshing or establishing their understanding of the research around the specific goal, often turning to their trusty friend, Google Scholar. The hope is to read a few relevant studies and journal articles (not every page, but enough to understand current literacy research on a practice) to be as centered on research as possible. They can share kernels of this research with teachers during co-planning to support the use of research-supported practices.

2. **More Personal Planning Time.** Coaches and teachers co-plan things like the lesson content, student tasks, and coaching support, but that isn't the *only* planning that happens. Coaches must plan their work more thoroughly, collecting student materials and asking themselves questions such as:

   ▓ "What will I ask the teacher to pay particular attention to during this portion of the lesson?" (when coach is modeling)

   ▓ "How will I facilitate reflection on the decisions made during instruction so we can replicate the in-the-moment teacher moves that positively impacted student learning?" (when the coach is co-teaching or observing).

3. **Organizing Data and Planning to Share.** As coaches collect observations and data, they will need time to review for patterns and recommendations. This work is needed to ensure organized coaching conferences. Spending time with observational and formative assessment data across lessons allows the coach to generate ideas about what might be replicated and what might change as instruction progresses. This allows the coach to be nimbler in coaching conferences, offering several promising options for the teacher to choose from as they plan their next instructional steps together.

Tools That Support Clear Communication

Let's consider tools that support key coaching and collaboration activities during the various stages of a coaching cycle. Then we will see ways these tools and processes were put to use with unique situations in real schools.

▓ **Conferencing to Set a Goal for the Coaching Cycle.** At the start of a coaching cycle, a coach works with a teacher or a team of teachers to refine the instructional goal so the work together will be intentional and measurable. Sometimes it's helpful to talk through the present state and desired state in relation to a general goal to help specify the focus of the coaching cycle. A resource like the sample form shown in Figure 3–10 helps guide the goal setting conversation. Although not always needed, tools

FIGURE 3–10 *Goal Setting Template*

GOAL SETTING: Considering the Present State and the Desired State

Consider your general goal. What does this currently look like in your context? What do you wish it would look like?

PRESENT STATE	DESIRED STATE

How would work toward this goal align with one or more learning standards?

How would work toward this goal align with a school or district goal/initiative (e.g., school improvement plan)?

What steps would help you move from the present state to the desired state? These steps could include expansion of knowledge, selection/development of materials, observation of instruction, implementation of instruction. Approximately how much time might each step take?

How could we most effectively work on the first step together? (What exactly will each of us do? What materials will we need to start? What will our time frame for this step be?)

like this can be used flexibly to land on a goal that addresses the right focus for the collaboration and clearly outlines the work ahead for the coach and teacher(s) alike.

- **Co-planning for Modeling.** When the teacher and coach identify that modeling would be beneficial, there are several things to think through together ahead of time that make for a smooth experience with students. The form in Figure 3–11 could be used to guide the co-planning conversation before a modeling experience. Forms like this work as a "third point," bringing focus and structure to a conversation, but also allowing modification when needed. When time allows, the teacher can prepare for the co-planning conversation by thinking through some of these questions ahead of time.

Forms work as a "third point," bringing focus and structure to a conversation.

- **Co-planning Lesson Template.** When it comes to the actual co-planning of the lesson, the coach and teacher will probably use some type of lesson plan template. One sample template that the pair can use to plan specifics can be seen in Figure 3–12. Often the coach will fill out the top portion and any details the teacher has already shared to save time during the co-planning conference.

- **Observation Guide.** Having a structured way to take notes when the other partner is the lead teacher supports meaningful conversations later. There are many simple ways that educators choose to take notes during a modeling session or a lesson observation. The sample form (Figure 3–13) allows flexibility for note taking and also provides ideas for two different types of conferences that can be used when discussing the observational data.

Not All Coaching Cycles Look Alike

As you will read in the following examples, coaching cycles do not always follow the traditional pattern of goal setting, co-planning, modeling, co-teaching, observation, and goal revisiting. Although

FIGURE 3–11 *Template for Planning a Modeled Lesson*

MODELING PLANNING TEMPLATE	
Purpose for Modeling	▶ I want the coach to develop and model a lesson that will allow me to learn . . . ▶ Specific questions or concerns I have are . . .
Learning Standards	▶ What learning standard(s) will the modeled lesson address? ▶ What do I want to see in the lesson related to the standard(s)?
Lesson Ideas	▶ What is the objective for the lesson? ▶ What have the students already done around this objective? ▶ Are there specific materials the coach should use in the lesson? If so, what are they? ▶ Will the lesson be taught to the whole class or to a small group? If a small group, why was that group selected? ▶ Are there other considerations that the coach should have in mind when planning the modeled lesson (e.g., time for the lesson, location of the lesson, classroom routines)?
Teacher Observation	▶ What specific things should I take notes about while observing the lesson? Have we developed an observation form that will help gather this information? ▶ When will I meet with the coach to discuss this lesson?

FIGURE 3–12 *Template for Co-Planning Lessons*

LESSON PLAN TEMPLATE
Teacher: Grade: Coach:
Date for Lesson:
Purpose or objective of lesson:
What will the students be able to do as a result of the lesson?
What academic vocabulary will be emphasized during the lesson?
Instructional Steps by Teacher and Students Note where teacher is providing explicit explanation (EE), modeling (M), guided practice (GP), or independent practice (IP). If this will be a co-taught lesson, put a T next to the activities that will be taught by the teacher and a C next to the activities that will be taught by the coach.

Teacher	Students

What materials are needed?

Assessment: How will you know that the students have met the expectations?

How will the coach support you with the lesson?

When will you and the coach meet to discuss the lesson?

FIGURE 3–13 *Template for Observation and Conferencing*

OBSERVATION GUIDE/CONFERENCING NOTES

Teacher: _____ Grade: _____ Date: _____

Lesson/Activity Observed: _____

Observation Focus: _____

Data About Observation Focus

Conference Details	**Next Steps for the Students**
1. Coach shares data with teacher and supports teacher reflection about the data by asking open-ended questions such as:	
a. How are these data similar to or different from what you expected?	
b. What factors may have influenced the observed data?	
Or	
2. Coach asks teacher to share their thoughts about the observation focus and then shares the data—showing how the data confirm or are different from teacher's observations. Coach supports teacher reflection about the data.	**Next Steps for the Teacher and Coach**

all cycles should start with an articulated goal and include some co-planning, the other activities in the cycle should be based on the decisions made collaboratively by the teacher and coach.

Following are some specific ways coaches and teachers have enacted coaching cycles to fit their school structures, their needs, and their unique situations. We will explore:

- short coaching cycles when coaching is new to a school,

- coaching that moves from light to deeper coaching cycles, and

- coaching cycles around district initiatives or school-wide goals.

Short Coaching Cycles When Coaching Is New to a School

When I became the first literacy coach in my district in 2004, I was unsure how to start working with my colleagues. My principal and I developed an approach that involved short coaching cycles where I was able to work with three teachers each month, for one hour a day each, five days a week. This plan was designed to help all eighteen first- through third-grade teachers have a positive, student-centered collaboration with a coach in the first six months of the program. Since each teacher and I set feasible goals and carefully designed our work together, we were pleased to see student learning data improve in the areas specifically related to our goals—and this happened in every first- through third-grade classroom that year!

Although working with each teacher for a predetermined period of time is probably not a model that would work year after year, it was a helpful way to build confidence and enthusiasm about coaching in our building. This strong foundation enabled us, in subsequent years, to be more systematic in focusing our coaching efforts on school-wide needs.

Let's see how a typical coaching cycle worked during those four-week collaborations with teachers.

Goal Setting

Our first couple of days were spent backward planning to design our month together. I used a simplified planning template to help us develop reasonable, data-based, and standards-aligned goals (see Figure 3–14).

Co-Planning

Once a goal was identified, we co-planned our coaching activities. We generally relied on the gradual release of responsibility, with me modeling the instructional practice the first week, the teacher and I co-teaching the second and third weeks, and the teacher implementing the instruction with me observing the last week.

Implementation

As we moved through our implementation, we committed to having a conference after each time we were in the classroom together, which is something that can be difficult to hold to when coaching is new. We would use these conferences to have reflective conversations about the last lesson and to co-plan the next task together.

Having a predictable set of questions to guide us helped make the coaching conversations more comfortable and purposeful.

Having a predictable set of questions to guide us helped make the coaching conversations more comfortable and purposeful (see Figure 3–15). I learned quickly that I did better when adhering to the flow of the questions on the form; otherwise, we could quickly lose our focus and engage in tangential conversations. This form is an alternate planning template to Figure 3-13. Coaches and teachers can choose the form that provides the best guidance to meet their needs.

FIGURE 3–14 *Planning for Coaching Cycles*

BRAINSTORMING PLANNING **Form for Coaching Cycles**

Student Needs

What are some ways students are having success with the literacy learning?

What are some of your students' specific literacy needs that might be puzzling? What data inform this?

What could we do together to meet one of those needs?

Instructional Needs

With what literacy instruction or practices do you want more experience or information?

With what student learning standards do you feel you would like more instructional support?

Shared Literacy Instructional Priorities to Keep in Mind

☐ Does the instruction align with student learning standards?

☐ Does the instruction we are planning align with research-supported practices?

☐ Does the instruction planned provide both explicit explanation *and* time for students to practice applying in real reading or writing?

FIGURE 3–15 *Planning Meeting Template for Reflection and Planning*

Planning Meeting Template

Who: _____

Date: _____

Time: _____

1. Debrief the last session together. "So we did this . . . and the students . . . and we noticed . . ."

2. Share our metacognition. What were we thinking as we taught? Did we change anything as we taught? Would we change anything if we had to do it over?

3. What was the outcome? Did we meet the student learning goal for the lesson? How will this help us plan the next steps we need to take with students?

4. Plan next steps. What is our plan for the next session together? Who will be doing what? What evidence of student learning do we expect to see? How will we record this?

Moving from Light Coaching to Deeper Coaching Cycles

Coaching cycles can sometimes start with a simple teacher request. One example of this is when Christine, who was new to second grade and new to the building, asked if LeMar, the literacy coach, could support her in designing her new classroom space and in using the resources available to her. Here's how their work together followed a coaching cycle.

Goal Setting and Co-Planning

LeMar gladly scheduled a first conference to learn more about Christine's immediate needs and then suggested a plan to meet those needs. First, he would help Christine make initial classroom design decisions—including student accessibility to a variety of resources—before school started. Then, during the third week of school, they would meet to reflect on how students were using the classroom texts and support materials to determine possible changes to the environment. LeMar created a chart for them to use to reflect on the current literacy environment and to set clear goals.

Christine and LeMar each filled out the chart independently and then compared their charts, talking about the differences in their notations. Christine found this process supportive and straightforward. As a result of their discussion, she set two goals: getting more texts related to students' interests into the room and learning how to make good use of the appropriate digital resources already available for her students.

Implementation

LeMar worked closely with Christine to find texts that she could purchase with a small grant from the community foundation. He also supported her decision-making around how and when to incorporate the digital resources. Later, Christine asked if they could continue to work on another category from the chart: developing appropriate routines in a social and literacy-rich learning environment. They planned out a more traditional coaching cycle that included modeling, co-teaching, and observing.

So, across a couple of months, a low-risk process of setting up a classroom led to more work together. A successful lighter level of support around resources turned into a deeper, more collaborative coaching cycle around research-supported instructional practices.

Coaching Cycles Around District Initiatives or School-Wide Goals

Many schools have district-level or school-level literacy leadership teams. A literacy coach is a valuable member of the literacy leadership team. To minimize "random acts of coaching," a school team can provide direction for some of the work a coach supports across the grade levels. Let's look at the way Corrine, a literacy coach who is new to the school, partnered with her colleagues on the literacy leadership team to develop the school-wide literacy goals and coaching focus for the year. See Figure 3–16.

FIGURE 3–16 *Observation Informs School-Wide Goal Setting and Coaching Focus*

A FOUR-STEP PROCESS
1. Observation, Reflection, and Planning
▶ Corrine studied student learning data and scheduled time to observe in each classroom, communicating with teachers that the goal of the observation was to identify school-wide themes and a general understanding of the literacy environment, instructional practices, and student learning.
▶ Corrine met with the building leadership team—composed of the principal, one teacher per grade level, and the district curriculum director—to determine a school-wide literacy goal.

2. Leadership Team Sets the Goal

▶ The leadership team articulated the school-wide literacy goal to the staff and presented ideas on how coaching could help achieve the goal.

▶ The team invited feedback from the teachers through reflective writing and a short survey.

Based on this feedback, the school-wide goal was refined to the following: *Use focused observation to guide targeted instruction with small groups and individual students.*

3. Goal Setting and Co-Planning with Grade-Level Teams

▶ In grade-level meetings, Corrine and teachers developed *grade-level areas of focus* related to the school's overall literacy goal.

▶ For example, Corrine supported the third-grade teachers as they made decisions about the student learning they would track and ways they would document that learning with the tool they created.

4. Goal Setting, Co-Planning, and Implementation with Individual Teachers

▶ Corrine scheduled a co-planning session with one of the third-grade teachers who wanted to specifically concentrate on how to use the data they had collected to plan individual conferences while students read in small groups.

Corrine not only helped them map out their conference topics, but also modeled several student conferences and observed as they conducted some conferences.

Overall, this school utilized a leadership team to create a systematized approach to coaching that allowed for a structured, unified focus as a whole school, while also providing flexibility and choice to meet specific groups and individual teachers at their point of need. Teachers noted that ongoing informal assessments showed student learning growth. In addition, grade level teams were pleased that they had created tools to support their current and future instructional planning.

Matching Goals and Priorities to Coaching Cycles

Some cycles are short and based on a simple question a teacher wishes to answer. These cycles may require only a co-planning session and a conference after the teacher implements the plan. Some cycles are long as the teacher strives to enhance a challenging instructional practice. These cycles may include several iterations of modeling, co-teaching, and observation. No matter the length of a coaching cycle, intentionality frames every decision coaches and teachers make. When they have the flexibility to decide their own purpose and duration for coaching cycles, revising as they go, coaches and teachers can maximize their time together for the greatest benefit to their students.

Coaching Schedules Reveal Priorities

Without a framework or guidelines for how they spend their time, sometimes newer coaches shape their schedules around whatever teacher requests come in, moving from one random need to the next. They do this with the best intentions, but it can leave them at the end of the day wondering what was accomplished to impact teaching and learning over time.

When I began as a coach, I thought that I should always say "yes" to teacher requests because if I could get a foot in the door, my colleagues would trust my support and keep that door open to want to engage in more research-supported coaching activities. I realize now that teachers are eager to work with a coach when they see the direct impact on student learning. Focusing most of our time in research-supported coaching activities *is* still responsive to teacher needs. We can keep in mind Susan's advice: To have the greatest impact on student learning, coaches are intentional with their time and focused on systematic, reliable coaching activities.

Mining Intentional Coaching Out of Randomness

Figure 3–17 provides ways to think about how random requests can become opportunities for more intentional coaching cycles.

FIGURE 3–17 *From Random to Intentional Coaching*

RANDOM ACTS OF COACHING	RESULTING INTENTIONAL COACHING
Organizing classroom libraries with teachers	Goal: To help students select appropriate independent reading materials and to help teachers engage in productive conferences with students about their independent reading
Finding resources requested by a teacher about a specific comprehension strategy	Goal: To use the gradual release of responsibility model (explicit explanation, modeling, collaborative practice, guided practice, independent practice [Duke et al. 2011]) so students can independently apply a small set of comprehension strategies when reading for academic and recreational purposes
Modeling an interactive read-aloud lesson requested by the teacher	Goal: To support the teacher in: ► learning about the purposes for interactive read-aloud, ► co-planning interactive read-aloud lessons, and ► co-teaching and independently teaching read-aloud lessons.
Answering a question about a new curricular resource	Goal: To work together to examine the curricular resource and its alignment with: ► the learning standards, ► research-supported practices, and ► student needs.

Controlling Our Coaching Schedules

Coaches, just like teachers and principals, are extremely busy, but there are some ways to gain a clearer understanding about where all the time goes. First, coaches can do a simple time analysis of their last typical week of work. See Figure 3–18.

FIGURE 3–18 *Coaching Time Analysis*

1. **Looking across each day in a week, assign each chunk of time on your calendar to categories such as:**

   a. working with teachers (e.g., coaching, grade-level meetings, and professional learning sessions),

   b. preparation for working with teachers,

   c. leadership activities such as committee meetings, organizing curricular resources, or planning summer literacy programs,

   d. personal professional development, and

   e. other office or managerial tasks.

2. **Count up the number of minutes roughly spent in each category.** Some people like copying their week's schedule and using highlighters to color-code each category as they sort their tasks.

3. **Next divide each category's total minutes by the average number of working minutes in a week (minus things like lunch time) to determine the percentage of time spent on each category.**

4. **Sketch a rough pie graph that shows how your time was spent in each area.** You may choose to blend the categories of working with teachers and preparation for working with teachers together into one category. This blended category should be more than half of your pie because research indicates that student learning is positively impacted when coaches spend a majority of the time with teachers.

5. **How did you do prioritizing time with teachers?** It's eye-opening to see an entire week of time distilled into one simple graphic. Coaches can use this quick process to set goals for themselves and their time. If they find they are not spending enough time with teachers, coaches could make a commitment to change one key thing about their coaching activities for the next week. They then do this quick graphing once a week for a few weeks in a row to gather more data and determine if the change(s) they made increased the amount of time spent with teachers.

6. **Coaches can also work together to brainstorm solutions to common problems.** They might choose to share their pie graph with another coach to ask for feedback on the priorities it seems to show. Some coaches choose to share the pie graph with an administrator to problem-solve areas of concern, thinking through new ways to shift or discontinue managerial tasks that take too much time away from working with teachers.

Figure 3–19 provides a sample schedule that is shaded to show the time categories for one coach's week. This coach, through reflection over time, was able to minimize managerial tasks in service to more time with teachers. His pie chart would show over half of his time spent working with and/or planning his work with teachers, a fifth of his time engaging in leadership activities, and an eighth of his time focused on his own professional development.

It is important to note that quality coaching requires planning time. In this sample week, twenty percent of the coach's time was spent in planning and preparation for coaching and leadership activities. Also, sometimes coaches put their needs last, which is a recipe for burnout. This coach has prioritized time for their own professional learning and reflection, showing that they understand the need to remain current about research-supported practices.

FIGURE 3–19 *Maximizing Time with Teachers*

	Monday	Tuesday	Wednesday	Thursday	Friday
9:00 a.m.	Observe Teacher A implement a vocabulary lesson	Analyze second-grade student data and prepare for second-grade team meeting	Model vocabulary lesson for Teacher A	Observe Teacher A implement vocabulary lesson	Facilitate second-grade team meeting
10:00 a.m.	Plan Wednesday's school English language arts meeting	Model vocabulary-focused interactive read-aloud lesson for Teacher B		Co-teach vocabulary-focused interactive read-aloud lesson with Teacher B	Co-teach vocabulary-focused interactive read-aloud lesson with Teacher B
11:00 a.m.			Prepare for kindergarten team meeting	Weekly meeting with principal	Facilitate kindergarten team meeting
12:00 p.m.	Lunch and prep for debrief with Teacher A	Lunch and prep for debrief with Teacher B	Lunch and read literature on English language learners	Lunch with Teacher E to discuss materials for upcoming unit	Coaches' professional learning community meeting (includes lunch)
1:00 p.m.	Debrief with Teacher A about vocabulary lesson	Participate in district literacy curriculum meeting	Debrief with Teacher A and co-plan next two vocabulary lessons	Debrief with Teacher A about the vocabulary lesson	
2:00 p.m.	Read literature on teacher leadership		Teach in Teacher C's room so she can observe Teacher D implement an interactive read-aloud lesson		Meet with Teacher C to discuss her observation of an interactive read-aloud lesson in Teacher D's class

	Monday	Tuesday	Wednesday	Thursday	Friday
3:00 p.m.	Building leadership team meeting	Debrief with Teacher B and co-plan next two vocabulary-focused interactive read-alouds	Gather materials for co-teaching vocabulary-focused interactive read-aloud lessons with Teacher B	Goal setting conference with Teacher F	Debrief vocabulary-focused interactive read-aloud lessons with Teacher B
4:00 p.m.		Prepare materials for modeling a vocabulary lesson in Teacher A's room	Facilitate school English language arts meeting	Gather sample nonfiction books that could be used for interactive read-alouds	Write weekly coaching reflection

Working with teachers—40%	Preparation for working with teachers—18%	Leadership activities, including preparation—20%	Personal professional development activities—13%

Helping Others Become Literacy Leaders

Do you know anyone who models a constant sense of wonder? Jane is that person. Jane is an experienced coach who is driven by

Coaches can help teachers turn anxiety into wonder and wonder into confident literacy leadership.

an innate curiosity and cares about how to motivate that same sense of inquiry in her teaching colleagues. Some teachers are anxious and facing burnout in our field. Jane has a gift for turning anxiety into wonder and wonder into confident literacy leadership. She and other coaches consistently use a few strategies to lift more leaders around them. They are 100 percent focused on

working themselves out of a job, knowing that shared leadership is exponentially more impactful than being the perceived expert.

Co-Facilitating Professional Learning

Jane often asks teachers to co-present with her during large-group professional learning sessions. Frequently these teachers have been a part of a coaching cycle with Jane to refine a particular practice or have achieved considerable student success with an instructional strategy. Before Jane co-presents with teachers, she meets with them to co-design not only the content that they will share, but also the exact protocols and activities that will support successful adult learning.

During the co-planning stage, she asks things like:

- "How do we know this is relevant for our participants?"

- "How will we emphasize the relevancy?"

- "OK, so as a participant, how would *you* appreciate reflecting on this content?"

- "What was one of the most motivating sessions you've attended? How do we get to that level of value for our colleagues in this session?"

With all of these layers of support, Jane empowers a teacher who might previously have been too cautious to co-present. Then, after the professional learning session, Jane debriefs with the teacher leader. Through reflection on what worked, the teacher's skills and confidence are strengthened even more.

Grade-Level Facilitation

When building capacity at the grade level, a coach might use a gradual release of responsibility model to transfer responsibility for facilitating grade-level meetings. For example, Conrad, a third-year coach, had the goal to develop Sarah's leadership skills in data analysis. Conrad facilitated the first data analysis meeting fully, using a data analysis protocol. For the second data analysis meeting, Conrad met with Sarah before the meeting to discuss the data. Then, during the grade-level meeting, Sarah facilitated the data analysis with her colleagues with Conrad supporting her by asking questions or adding comments as needed. After the meeting, Conrad and Sarah collaboratively reflected on her facilitation. Sarah facilitated the next data meeting with Conrad completing a facilitation observation sheet that he and Sarah had developed together. Then, using Conrad's notes, they discussed Sarah's leadership skills and what, if any, support she would need during future data analysis meetings.

Teachers Sharing Their Practice

Many teams in schools use processes like facilitated classroom visits or video recording for team reflection. A coach's role in such a process is to facilitate and model nonjudgmental reflection on teaching practices and student learning with other educators. After the coach initiates these interclassroom observations and discussions, it is common for teachers to then take the leadership in inviting others to visit their classrooms to observe specific literacy practices. Teachers use several methods to indicate when others may come in and watch teaching and learning in action. Whether a chart in the supply room indicating the days and lessons open for visitors or a sign outside of the class door welcoming others in, this trend toward sharing teaching is a powerful example of what can happen when the barriers of worry are washed away with supported teacher risk-taking. Processes like this help teachers more regularly and flexibly open the doors of their practice to each other. Curiosity and motivation for this kind of collaboration can become contagious.

Collaboration Between Coaches and Principals

Collaborations are built on effective communication, and the work between a principal and literacy coach is no exception.

Clear Coaching Responsibilities

Because coaching is still a fairly new position in some school systems, a clear job description provides clarity and confidence for all involved. Coaches need job descriptions that explicitly outline research-supported roles, responsibilities, and teacher-focused priorities listed in Figure 2–2 on page 19. When administrators and coaches hold the same understanding for the coaching role, it helps the coach work with purpose and focus. Then, as the principals regularly share their excitement for the coaching role with staff, they are able to speak with positive examples and specific priorities—as seen in the example below.

Coaches need job descriptions that outline research-supported roles, responsibilities, and teacher-focused priorities.

Most principals reinforce the roles and responsibilities of the coach at the beginning of each year. During this discussion, principals encourage teachers to ask questions. Teachers frequently ask questions like, "Is the coach only working with new teachers or are you assigning the coach to work with teachers who have problems?" A research-based response to this question might sound like, "The answer is simple. No, the coach is not assigned to teachers. The coach has autonomy to create a schedule based on whole-staff, small-group, and individual teachers' areas of focus and requests. If we as a school are learning something new, the coach will facilitate whole-staff professional learning or support a group of teachers to facilitate the professional learning. In some cases, the coach will work with a group of teachers in the grade level where student need is the greatest to problem-solve and help adjust instruction. Or, if a grade-level team is piloting a new instructional resource or practice, some coaching support will be provided to the group based on the team's goal, and some coaching work will come about through requests from individual teachers. Coaching support is diverse, but the goals you will develop with the coach always will be based on enhancing student learning."

When the principal takes the lead on initial staff communication about the coaching role and responsibilities, the coach is able to quickly move into the day-to-day work with teachers because everyone holds the same basic understanding about the collaboration. The coach doesn't have to repeatedly introduce the role to individual staff members, slowing down the work at the beginning of the year. All staff members understand the purpose of the coaching role and confusion is minimized. A clear job description also helps an eager-to-serve coach prioritize time around the activities that will *most* impact student learning outcomes. Detailed coaching responsibilities allow a coach to make decisions that avoid "random acts of coaching" which will not have an impact on student learning.

What Teachers Want to Know About the Coach-Principal Relationship

We frequently hear coaches say that teachers do not have a clear understanding of the role of the coach. Coaches have shared some common questions that teachers or principals ask them about coaching and the communication between the coach and principal. It would be valuable for the principal to discuss these topics with the staff at the beginning of the year to successfully set the literacy coaching plan into motion.

Coach and Principal Meetings

To align systems, goals, and supports, a principal and literacy coach will want to establish and define the frequency and nature of their collaboration. Prioritize time on your calendars at least once every two weeks for this one-on-one collaboration. This time will be fruitful, especially if the coach sends a list of conversation topics prior to the meetings so the principal is able to prepare any thoughts and questions. To avoid "random acts of coaching" and "random acts of literacy leadership," a coach and principal will do well to hold this collaborative time together as a valuable nonnegotiable in their work.

Regular topics of conversation include:

- progress toward school-wide literacy goals,

- themes emerging from the ongoing coaching,

- plans for future professional learning, and

- co-learning that is prioritized to enhance principal and, at times, coach expertise in a specific area of literacy learning.

Here is one caution about the coach and principal conversations: they should not include discussion of individual teachers. Coaching is based on trusting relationships with teachers. This trust is fragile—especially at the beginning of a coaching initiative. Part of this trust comes from knowing that coaches are not evaluators and that coaches will maintain confidentiality about their interactions with teachers. Therefore, when meeting together for any purpose, it is important that the coach and principal follow the norm that they simply will not discuss individual teachers. When principals originally explain this aspect of the process to a staff member, some teachers ask if it is okay for the teachers to share with the principal what they are working on with the coach. The principal could answer, "Yes, it is perfectly acceptable for you as a teacher to talk with me about your work with the literacy coach. Just remember that I will not be sharing any of your comments with the coach—nor will the coach share anything with me about your specific work together."

Let's consider some examples to highlight open, flexible, yet confidential communication between the coach and the principal. Because teachers are key players in the coaching program, these examples focus on the ways that a coach, principal, and teacher discuss the coaching program and its results. See Figure 3–20.

Enhancing Principal Knowledge

No matter the level of experience of a principal, the collaboration between a coach and principal often includes learning together to continue to develop the principal's literacy expertise. Although the principal of a school does not need to be an expert on every aspect of literacy, some key literacy areas may be priorities for deeper learning so principals can conduct quality classroom observation and make informed decisions about future professional development topics.

These learning needs vary for each principal, but they might include ways teachers can increase engagement in reading and writing, examples of research-supported flexible grouping options, and structures for using observation and assessment in the everyday planning for instruction.

In some cases, the areas that the principal wants to learn more about are also areas that the coach needs to learn more about, as coaches—especially beginning coaches—cannot be expected to have expertise in all aspects of literacy development. In these cases, the coach and principal would be peer learners, choosing learning modes and materials to best meet their needs.

After a principal and coach identify an area for further learning, a literacy coach might:

■ **Invite the principal to come see the coach model a variety of lessons in different classrooms.** The coach could provide a handout listing what the principal should be seeing, and, after the lesson, have a conversation about the instruction and student learning observed during the lesson.

FIGURE 3–20 *Examples of Coach, Principal, and Teacher Talk About Coaching*

CONVERSATIONS	WHY THE CONVERSATION IS PRODUCTIVE
Literacy coach to principal: "I'm looking forward to supporting the third-grade team with their new goal. We've been looking at student writing together, and we are noticing some common needs across the classrooms that could be addressed with some intentional small-group instruction. I will support the team next week when they plan some of these small groups together, each teacher creating a plan for a specific group of students and sharing the plans across the grade level. I'll check in with individual teachers as they get started and make myself available to co-plan, observe, or model as needed."	The coach is catching the principal up on new work based on student learning goals. Note: The coach is not discussing their work with individual teachers.
Teacher to principal: "I'm astonished at the students' writing engagement lately. Ever since we've been working on helping students set goals and working together in small groups, their talk during writing time has been so purposeful. They don't want writing time to stop!"	The teacher is celebrating student learning with the principal.
Principal to literacy coach: "You shared with me the last time we talked how one grade level is examining student writing to create small-group plans. How could I support this? Do you think that team would be ready to share their process with other grade levels? We have a staff meeting later this month. I know two other grade levels that have discussed similar goals and might really appreciate hearing from others who are finding success looking at student writing. What do you think? If the group thinks it is too soon, we will wait."	The principal is supporting the coaching work and thinking of ways to build capacity across grade levels. Note: The principal is not asking about the coach's work with individual teachers.
Principal to staff at faculty meeting: "In my meetings with Tamina, she has shared her main coaching areas of support for this quarter, including one team's plan to examine student writing to set goals. The teachers also shared with me their efforts around small-group writing instruction based on their observations of student work. Today, they are excited to share their process, look at some student work together, and get some wider feedback from the rest of us."	The principal is publicly supporting coaching and providing time for teachers to share and seek feedback from each other with a focus on student learning.

- **Invite the principal to attend and actively participate in the professional learning the coach is facilitating for a small group or large group of teachers.** As with the modeling, the coach should follow up by scheduling a conversation with the principal to process the learning and answer any questions and discuss next steps.

- **Attend a local or state professional development session about some aspect of research-supported literacy instruction with the principal and possibly one or two teachers from the building.** Following this collaborative learning, the team could continue to meet to identify how to share the new learning with the whole staff in ways that fit within the school's literacy plan and practices.

- **Go with the principal to another building to observe strong practices related to an identified aspect of literacy, with opportunities to discuss observations together.** The key in this option is to visit another school and to not observe together in your own building. Coaching is not evaluative. If a coach and principal were to observe together in their own building, they might give the impression that the coach is involved in the evaluation process. Also, visiting a new school provides a change of pace that allows for deeper reflection and processing.

Coaches and principals who continue to learn themselves lead by example.

These examples are only some of the ways a coach and principal could engage in new learning together. Prioritizing time for continued learning and collaboration around literacy practices establishes the importance of ongoing, goal-based professional learning. Coaches and principals who continue to learn themselves lead by example, enhancing a school culture of professional efficacy and continuous improvement.

Ongoing Professional Learning for Coaches

So much can compete for a coach's time. It is easy to set goals for continuous learning, but—in the rush of daily work—find the journal articles getting dusty on the desk as we unintentionally put our needs last. Dr. Nell K. Duke reminds us that education should be more like the medical field. Would we go to a doctor who was out of touch with the current science of her field? As with medicine, it's detrimental to our students if we ignore the growing body of literacy research when making decisions in our work. The following questions, adapted from *Standards for the Preparation of Literacy Professionals 2017* (International Literacy Association 2018), may help coaches self-assess their ongoing learning. Jotting down specific examples related to each question may help determine areas of strength and need. Coaches could use this self-assessment to build goals and action steps for their professional learning.

> How am I staying current with my knowledge about the research around language acquisition, reading, writing, and topics specific to my school?

> When designing professional learning, do I consistently consider adult learning principles such as providing choice, ensuring relevance to teachers' real work, and providing time to plan application and next steps?

> How have I successfully collaborated with teachers in creating, analyzing, transforming, and implementing diverse learning experiences that are culturally responsive and link school, home, and community literacy knowledge?

> Am I able to administer, score, and use the results of the literacy assessments given in my school to make decisions about instruction?

> Am I able to identify and design research-supported components of a literacy-rich learning environment?

> Do I regularly reflect on my work; act as a critical consumer of research, policy, and practices; and share findings with others?

Belief in Continuous Improvement

Building efficacy as a group of educators is, in part, about coordination of beliefs and actions. If we *believe* in the potential of our colleagues to create significant student growth, our *actions* will be in line with that belief. One outgrowth of these clear actions and beliefs will be the *intentionality* with which we make our choices as we work together. We will intentionally partner with others to solve problems of practice. We will engage in coordinated inquiry to work toward new goals together. We will accomplish these goals because we believe we are capable when working together. We will realize we need each other to accomplish our goals more quickly.

So, what *do* we believe about our colleagues? Just like our beliefs about our students, our trust in the capacity of those around us can be revised and replenished. Literacy coaching provides a fresh hope and a means to accelerate our capacity as educators. As we dive into new levels of collaboration, we won't be focusing as much on what we do individually. Instead, we will put more energy and focus into what we can do to improve all students' learning . . . together.

AFTERWORD

Nell K. Duke

I have argued that being a classroom teacher may be just as complex as being an emergency room (ER) physician (Duke 2019). Like ER physicians, teachers need lots of content knowledge (e.g., specific kinds of letter-sound relationships in English orthography, how humans acquire vocabulary knowledge). They also need many skills for applying that content knowledge (e.g., how to teach letter-sound relationships, how to teach vocabulary). And just as ER physicians need to interact effectively with their patients, teachers need to know how to interact effectively with—plus engage and motivate—their students. ER physicians need to attend to the needs of many patients, who have different backgrounds, strengths, and needs, in any given shift; classroom teachers need to attend to the needs of many students, who have different backgrounds, strengths, and needs, at any given moment. Arguably, classroom teachers are in a more difficult situation because they don't just see individuals one at a time, the way an ER physician would; rather, teachers are expected to address the needs of many students all at once.

To prepare for the complexity of their work as an ER physician, a prospective physician will typically obtain an undergraduate degree with a strong grounding in science. Then they will go through four years of medical school. Those four years are followed by three to four years of residency in which their work is carried out in close collaboration with one or more supervising mentors. In some cases additional specialized training follows.

To prepare for the complexity of their work as a classroom teacher, a prospective teacher will typically have approximately one and a half years of their undergraduate coursework directly correlate to their profession and approximately a half year of student teaching in which their work is carried out in close collaboration with one or more supervising mentors. Classroom teachers who go through alternative certification processes may have less of one or both of these forms of training.

I contend that these dramatic differences in the preparation of ER physicians and classroom teachers are not due to differences in the actual complexity of the work. Rather, they stem from differences in how society has viewed and valued these fields and the people who go into them.

What does all of this have to do with a book about coaching? It points to how absolutely critical teacher-coach collaboration is to teacher development and effectiveness. Cycles of coaching provide a concrete mechanism for teachers to continue to improve their practice and, in turn, to inform the work of the coach. At its best, teacher-coach collaborations help to compensate for some of the significant limitations of our initial teacher preparation system. Such collaborations also address the fact that new educational research is published every day. Just as we would not want ER physicians to rest on the knowledge they developed while in training without updating it as medical research yields new insights, so, too, do we want teachers to continue to refresh their practice as educational research advances.

Erin Brown and Susan L'Allier have both drawn on a significant body of research centered on coaching, as well as extensive professional experience, in writing this book. I hope it proves deeply useful to you as you design and refine coaching systems in your school. Whether a classroom teacher or a coach, your work is complex—as complex as that of many other professions—and you deserve the opportunity for ongoing professional collaboration to support you in developing in that work.

REFERENCES

Atteberry, A., and A. S. Bryk. 2011. "Participation in Literacy Coaching Activities." *The Elementary School Journal* 112 (2): 356–82.

Bean, R., and J. Lillenstein. 2012. "Response to Intervention and the Changing Roles of Schoolwide Personnel." *The Reading Teacher* 65 (7): 491–501.

Bean, R. M., B. Belcastro, J. Draper, V. Jackson, K. Jenkins, J. Vandermolen, N. Zigmond, and L. Kenavey. 2008. *Literacy Coaching in Reading First Schools: The Blind Men and the Elephant.* Paper presented at the National Reading Conference, Orlando, FL, December 4, 2008.

Bean, R. M., J.A. Draper, V. Hall, J. Vandermolen, and N. Zigmond. 2010. "Coaching in Reading First Schools: A Reality Check." *The Elementary School Journal* 111 (1): 87–114.

Bean, R. M., D. Kern, V. Goatley, E. Ortlieb, J. Shettel, K. Calo, et al. 2015. "Specialized Literacy Professionals as Literacy Leaders: Results of a National Survey." *Literacy Research and Instruction* 54 (2): 83–114.

Beck, I. L., and M. B. McKeown. 2006. *Improving Comprehension with Questioning the Author: A Fresh and Expanded View of a Powerful Approach.* New York: Scholastic.

Biancarosa, G., A. S. Bryk, and E. R. Dexter. 2010. "Assessing the Value-Added Effects of Literacy Collaborative Professional Development on Student Learning." *The Elementary School Journal* 111 (1): 7–34.

Bright, E., and T. Hensley. 2010. *A Study of the Effectiveness of K–3 Literacy Coaches.* (Department of Education Contract No. ED08-CO-0123). Portsmouth, NH: National Reading Technical Assistance Center.

Bryk, A. S., P. B. Sebring, E. Allensworth, S. Luppescu, and J. Q. Easton. 2010. *Organizing Schools for Improvement: Lessons from Chicago.* Chicago: University of Chicago Press.

Calo, K. M., E. G. Sturtevant, and K. M. Kopfman. 2015. "Literacy Coaches' Perspectives of Themselves as Literacy Leaders: Results from a National Study of K–12 Literacy Coaching and Leadership." *Literacy Research and Instruction* 54 (1): 1–18.

Camburn, E. M., S. M. Kimball, and R. Lowenhaupt 2008. "Going to Scale with Teacher Leadership: Lessons Learned from a District-wide Literacy Coach Initiative." In *Effective Teacher Leadership: Using Research to Inform and Reform*, edited by M. M. Mangin and S. R. Stoelinga, 120–43. New York: Teachers College Press.

Camburn, E., B. Rowan, and J. E. Taylor. 2003. "Distributed Leadership in Schools: The Case of Elementary Schools Adopting Comprehensive School Reform Models." *American Educational Research Association* 24 (4): 347–73.

Carlisle, J., and S. Berebitsky. 2011. "Literacy Coaching as a Component of Professional Development." *Reading and Writing* 24 (7): 773–800.

Desimone, L. M. 2009. "Improving Impact Studies of Teachers' Professional Development: Toward Better Conceptualizations and Measures." *American Educational Research Association* 38 (3): 181–99.

Deussen, T., T. Coskie, L. Robinson, and E. Autio. 2007. *"Coach" Can Mean Many Things: Five Categories of Literacy Coaches in Reading First* (Issues and Answers Report, REL 7007-No. 005). Washington, DC: U.S. Department of Education, Institute of Education Sciences, National Center for Education Evaluation and Regional Assistance, Regional Educational Laboratory Northwest.

Duke, N. K. 2019. "Reading by Third Grade: How Policymakers Can Foster Early Literacy." *The State Education Standard* 19 (2): 6–11.

Duke, N. K., P. D. Pearson, S. L. Strachan, and A. K. Billman. 2011. "Essential Elements of Fostering and Teaching Reading Comprehension." In *What Research Has to Say About Reading Instruction*, edited by S. J. Samuels and A. E. Farstrup, 51–93. Newark, DE: International Reading Association.

Elish-Piper, L., and S. L'Allier. 2010. "Exploring the Relationship Between Literacy Coaching and Student Reading Achievement in Grades K–1." *Literacy Research and Instruction* 49 (2): 162–74.

———. 2011. "Examining the Relationship Between Literacy Coaching and Student Reading Gains in Grades K–3." *The Elementary School Journal* 112 (1): 83–106.

———. 2014. *The Common Core Coaching Book: Strategies to Help Teachers Address the K–5 ELA Standards*. New York: Guilford.

Frost, S., and R. Bean. 2006. "Qualifications for Literacy Coaches: Achieving the Gold Standard." http://citeseerx.ist.psu.edu /viewdoc/download?doi=10.1.1.451.9687&rep=rep1& type=pdf. Accessed March 20, 2009.

Heineke, S. F. 2013. "Coaching Discourse: Supporting Teachers' Professional Learning." *The Elementary School Journal* 113 (3): 409–33.

International Literacy Association. 2018. *Standards for the Preparation of Literacy Professionals 2017*. Newark, DE: International Literacy Association.

Ippolito, J. 2010. "Three Ways That Literacy Coaches Balance Responsive and Directive Relationships with Teachers." *The Elementary School Journal* 111 (1): 164–90.

Kraft, M. A., D. Blazar, and D. Hogan. 2018. "The Effect of Teacher Coaching on Instruction and Achievement: A Meta-Analysis of the Causal Evidence." *Review of Educational Research* 88 (4): 547–88.

Lipton, L., and B. Wellman. 2007. "How to Talk so Teachers Listen." *Educational Leadership* 65 (1): 30–34.

Mangin, M. M. 2007. "Facilitating Elementary Principals' Support for Instructional Teacher Leadership." *Educational Administration Quarterly* 43 (3): 319–57.

Marsh, J. A., J. S. McCombs, J. R. Lockwood, F. Martorell, D. Gershwin, S. Naftel, et al. 2008. *Support Literacy Across the Sunshine State: A Study of Florida Middle School Reading Coaches*. Santa Monica, CA: RAND.

Matsumura, L. C., H. E. Garnier, R. Correnti, B. Junker, and D. D. Bickel. 2010. "Investigating the Effectiveness of a Comprehensive Literacy Coaching Program in Schools with High Teacher Mobility." *The Elementary School Journal* 111 (1): 35–62.

Matsumura, L. C., H. E. Garnier, and J. Spybrook. 2013. "Literacy Coaching to Improve Student Reading Achievement: A Multi-Level Mediation Model." *Learning and Instruction* 25: 35-48.

Matsumura, L. C., M. Sartoris, D. D. Bickel, and H. E. Garnier. 2009. "Leadership for Literacy Coaching: The Principal's Role in Launching a New Coaching Program." *Educational Administration Quarterly* 45 (5): 655–93.

McVee, M. B., E. Ortlieb, J. S. Reichenberg, and P. D. Pearson, eds. 2019. *The Gradual Release of Responsibility in Literacy Research and Practice*. Bingley, UK: Emerald Publishing Limited.

Neuman, S. B., and L. Cunningham. 2009. "The Impact of Professional Development and Coaching on Early Language and Literacy Instructional Practices." *American Educational Journal* 46 (2): 532–66.

Neuman, S. B., and T. S. Wright. 2010. "Promoting Language and Literacy Development for Early Childhood Educations: A Mixed-Methods Study of Coursework and Coaching." *The Elementary School Journal* 111 (1): 63–86.

Pearson, P. D., and M. Gallagher. 1983. "The Instruction of Reading Comprehension." *Contemporary Educational Psychology* 8: 317–344.

Rainville, K. N., and S. Jones. 2008. "Situated Identities: Power and Positioning in the Work of a Literacy Coach." *The Reading Teacher* 61 (6): 440–48.

Sailors, M., and L. Price. 2015. "Support for the Improvement of Practices Through Intensive Coaching (SIPIC): A Model of Coaching for Improving Reading Instruction and Reading Achievement." *Teaching and Teacher Education* 45: 115–27.

Stephens, D., D. N. Morgan, D. E. DeFord, A. Donnelly, E. Hamel, K. J. Keith, et al. 2011. "The Impact of Literacy Coaches on Teachers' Beliefs and Practices." *Journal of Literacy Research* 43 (3): 215–49.

Supovitz, J., P. Sirinides, and H. May. 2010. "How Principals and Peers Influence Teaching and Learning." *Educational Administration Quarterly* 46 (1): 31–56.

Taylor, B. M., and D. S. Peterson. 2006. *Year Three Report of the Minnesota Reading First Cohort 1 School Change Project*. St Paul, MN: University of Minnesota.

Taylor, B. M., D. S. Peterson, M. Marx, and M. Chein. 2007. "Scaling Up a Reading Reform in High-Poverty Elementary Schools." In *Effective Instruction for Struggling Readers K–6*, edited by B. M. Taylor and J. E. Ysseldyke, 216–34. New York: Teachers College Press.

Toll, C. A. 2006. *The Literacy Coach's Desk Reference*. Urbana, IL: National Council of Teachers of English.

Vanderburg, M., and D. Stephens. 2010. "The Impact of Literacy Coaches: What Teachers Value and How Teachers Change." *The Elementary School Journal* 111 (1): 141–63.

Walpole, S., M. C. McKenna, X. Uribe-Zarain, and D. Lamitina. 2010. "The Relationships Between Coaching and Instruction in the Primary Grades: Evidence from High-Poverty Schools." *The Elementary School Journal* 111 (1): 115–40.

Yoon, K. S., T. Duncan, S. W.-Y. Lee, B. Scarloss, and K. Shapley. 2007. *Reviewing the Evidence on How Teacher Professional Development Affects Student Achievement* (Issues and Answers Report, REL 2007–No. 033). Washington, DC: U.S. Department of Education, Institute of Education Sciences, National Center for Education Evaluation and Regional Assistance, Regional Educational Laboratory Southwest.